Jonas
Salk

Jonas Salk

MARJORIE CURSON

Silver Burdett Press
Englewood Cliffs, New Jersey

This book is dedicated to my hard-working father, with love.

CONSULTANTS

Kristie Ross
Ph.D. Candidate, History of Medicine/
   Nursing
Columbia University

Richard M. Haynes
Assistant Professor
Division of Administration, Curriculum,
   and Instruction
Western Carolina University

TEXT CREDITS:
Breakthrough: The Saga of Jonas Salk. © 1965 by Richard Carter. Reprinted by
permission of Trident Press, a division of Simon & Schuster, Inc.
Copyright © 1916/1965 by The New York Times Company. Reprinted by permission.
Man Unfolding (New York: Harper & Row) from pp. 70, 80. © 1972 by Jonas Salk.
Reprinted by permission of Jonas Salk.
Copyright 1953 Time Inc. Reprinted by permission.

PHOTOGRAPH ACKNOWLEDGMENTS:
AP/Wide World Photos: 88, 90, 95, 121; March of Dimes Birth Defects Foundation:
frontispiece, 9, 36, 56, 79, 85, 93, 105; UPI/Bettman Newsphotos: 5, 18, 49, 52, 107,
111, 115.

SERIES AND COVER DESIGN:
R STUDIO T Raúl Rodríguez and Rebecca Tachna

ART DIRECTOR:
Linda Huber

MANAGING EDITOR
Nancy Furstinger

PROJECT EDITOR:
Richard G. Gallin

PHOTO RESEARCH:
Omni-Photo Communications, Inc.

Published by Silver Burdett Press, Inc., a division of
Simon & Schuster, Inc., Englewood Cliffs, NJ 07632

Library of Congress Cataloging-in-Publication Data

Curson, Marjorie.
Jonas Salk / Marjorie Curson.
p. cm.—(Pioneers in change)
Includes bibliographical references.
Summary: A biography of the scientist who developed a vaccine that conquered polio.
1. Salk, Jonas, 1914- —Juvenile literature.   2. Virologists—
United States—Biography—Juvenile literature.   3. Poliomyelitis
vaccine—Juvenile literature.   [1. Salk, Jonas, 1914-
2. Scientists.   3. Poliomyelitis vaccine.]   I. Title. II. Series.
QR31.S25C87   1990
610.92—dc20
[B]   90-34463
[92]   CIP
                                                                 AC

Manufactured in the United States of America.
ISBN 0-382-09966-4 (lib. ed.)
10 9 8 7 6 5 4 3 2 1
ISBN 0-382-09971-0 (pbk.)
10 9 8 7 6 5 4 3 2 1

CONTENTS

1

The Disease Children Get

The story of Jonas Salk is the story of a brilliant young scientist and a terrible disease. It is also the story of a wise lawyer and a U.S. president who walked with crutches, forty summers of fear, hundreds of laboratories, thousands of small monkeys, and an organization with the strange name of the March of Dimes.

This message was on the front page of the *New York Times* on the morning of July 4, 1916.

INFANTILE PARALYSIS (POLIOMYELITIS)

Infantile paralysis is very prevalent [widespread] in this part of the city.

Keep your children out of the street as much as possible, and be sure to keep them out of the houses on which the Department of Health has put a sign.

The ... paper will tell you in what houses the disease is.

This is the disease which babies and young children get; many of them die, and many who do not become paralyzed [unable to move parts of their bodies] for life. Do not let your children go to parties, picnics, or outings.
If your child is sick, send for your doctor or notify the Board of Health.

This newspaper article was reprinted from a leaflet that New York City's Department of Health planned to hand out in parts of the city where many cases of infantile paralysis had been reported. The health authorities had printed 500,000 copies of the leaflet because there was an epidemic—a sudden, rapidly spreading outbreak—of infantile paralysis in New York City and all across the United States that summer.

Although infantile paralysis was not an unknown disease, it had never seemed a great threat to people before. No one was prepared for an epidemic. But 27,363 cases and 7,179 deaths were reported in 1916 in the twenty states where public health workers were required to keep track of such information. We will never know how many more cases there were in other states. New Yorkers suffered the most. A total of 9,023 cases were reported in the nation's largest city, and 2,448 of these people died.

The year 1916 was not a happy year to begin with. The same newspaper that carried the text of the Department of Health leaflet was filled with war news from Europe. The nations of Europe were engaged in a world war that had been going on since 1914. The United States did not send soldiers to the fighting until the winter of 1917. But in the spring of 1916 Americans were anxious and worried about the future.

Early in June, some cases of infantile paralysis were

reported on an inside page of the *New York Times*. By July, a column about the disease appeared regularly on page one. The numbers of new cases and deaths were given every day. For example, on July 13 there were 24 deaths and 117 new cases in the city. On July 15, there were 27 deaths and 144 new cases. On July 29, there were 44 deaths and 161 new cases. On August 3, there were 43 deaths and 217 new cases. On August 7, after some lower figures had been reported, 33 deaths and 193 new cases were noted, along with the news that the increase was "caused by heat."

Most of the sick people were children. But it soon became clear that people of all ages could get the disease mistakenly named *infantile paralysis*. *Infantile* means "of or related to young children or babies." Yet among the victims were many young adults in their teens and twenties.

What caused this disease? Nobody knew the answer, but it seemed as if everybody had an idea. Some people blamed pollution. Others suggested that the cause was dirt. On July 14, 355 New Yorkers were fined for breaking sanitary laws—laws designed to keep places clean and healthful. Still others were sure the disease was spread by animals. On July 25, the Society for the Prevention of Cruelty to Animals reported that hundreds of dogs and cats had been killed. Mosquitoes, flies, and fleas were blamed, then "second-hand material in bedding," then chickens, and then fish. The Anti-Vaccination League claimed vaccinations (injections, or shots, of antidisease material) for other diseases such as smallpox had caused the epidemic.

If no one was sure what spread infantile paralysis, how could the sickness be stopped? At that time, seriously ill people were usually quarantined. A notice was tacked to their front door, and they were not allowed to leave home until they were well again. In the summer of 1916, the victims of infantile paralysis were quarantined or sent to hospitals where they were kept away from the other patients. Healthy children in homes where people had taken sick were also quarantined.

Communities around New York City tried to prevent New Yorkers from entering their towns. Children without a health certificate that said they were well were not allowed to travel by train. Private automobiles with children in them were turned back if they tried to leave the city. Fear was everywhere.

Children were kept out of movie theaters. For a time, the New York Public Library closed its doors to children. A priest on Long Island told a newspaper reporter that some people were trying to keep children from going to his church.

Different organizations began to collect money to aid "cripples." The *New York Times* regularly carried word of contributions to "the brace fund." Braces made of metal and leather were used to support the paralyzed part of the body. John D. Rockefeller, one of the world's wealthiest men, donated a house to be used as an isolation hospital. There sick children could be kept away from others.

"These are dark days for parents," one editorial writer said. An earlier editorial had pointed out that people were acting in an hysterical manner. Other diseases claimed more young lives, the writer argued. But it was true that infantile paralysis was a very frightening disease. In particular, for a child to be paralyzed seemed to many people to be a fate worse than death.

That year the opening of school in New York City was put off for about a month. School finally began on September 25. On September 26 the newspaper listed only eleven deaths and twenty new cases. The epidemic was coming to

New York City. Jonas E. Salk was born in Manhattan in 1914.

an end. Still, someone suggested that classrooms should be sprayed with oil to protect the students from sickness.

Jonas Salk was almost two years old at the time of that first, unexpected infantile paralysis epidemic. Undoubtedly his parents were as worried as all the other mothers and fathers of young children living in New York City in the summer of 1916.

Jonas Edward Salk was born on October 28, 1914, in the part of New York that is called Manhattan. His parents, Daniel Bonn Salk and Dora Press Salk, were Jewish-American immigrants who had come to the United States from Russia. They both worked in the garment industry that produced ready-to-wear clothing. Daniel was a designer of women's neckwear and blouses. Jonas was the oldest of the Salks' three boys.

When Jonas was still small, the Salks moved to a neighborhood of small apartment houses in the Bronx, the northernmost part of the city. It was here that he attended elementary school and pleased his parents and teachers by learning quickly and eagerly. Years later, one of his early teachers remembered Jonas as a boy "who read everything that he could lay his hands on."

Daniel and Dora, better known as Dolly, wanted their firstborn son to take advantage of every opportunity the United States had to offer. They especially valued education. Fortunately, in the 1920s, in New York City, boys as promising as Jonas could get a good education for free. Of course, their families had to be willing to give up the money a teenager could earn if he or she went straight from grade school into a full-time job.

At the age of twelve, Jonas was accepted by a special school, the Townsend Harris High School. Established by the City College of New York (CCNY), this school was an experiment. It was free for students who were bright—and willing to finish a four-year course of study in three years. It was extremely difficult to get into Townsend Harris, and the class work was not easy. Every student was a good student! But Jonas thrived under this pressure. He was used to working hard in order to live up to his parents' high expectations. Competition spurred him on. He entered college according to plan, in 1929 when he was just fifteen years old—three years earlier than most starting students today!

October 28, 1929, was Jonas Salk's fifteenth birthday. The very next day the stock market crashed, and the Great Depression of the 1930s soon began. During the depression, banks and businesses failed, thousands of companies closed down, and many farmers lost their farms. There was a terrible drought in the Great Plains. Nearly one out of every four workers in the United States was out of work. In a way, this was not a bad time to go to school, because unemployment was so widespread that most people, old and young, experienced and inexperienced, had trouble finding work. The above-average intelligence that enabled Jonas to gain admission first to Townsend Harris, then to the City College of New York, also enabled him to get on with his life at a time when many young people failed to "make something of themselves."

What were Jonas Salk's hopes and dreams at this time? He was confident of his abilities, he enjoyed his studies, and he expected to become a lawyer one day. But he also had a plan in mind, an ambition that kept him going and always doing his best. It was Jonas's dream to be free to do his own work in his own way. And this dream was important to him.

Meanwhile, every spring brought with it a new outbreak of infantile paralysis, also called poliomyelitis—or polio, for short. These outbreaks were not as fierce as the epidemic of 1916, but they were just as sad for the victims and their families. Summertime, when people gathered together at parks, beaches, playgrounds, and swimming pools, became known as "the polio season."

Scientists believe poliomyelitis has been around for thousands of years. A picture made by ancient Egyptians shows a priest with a shrunken leg, walking on crutches.

The man who first called polio "spinal infantile paralysis" was a German physician (medical doctor) who worked with crippled people. In the early 1800s, he found that the disease attacked the spinal cords of small children. Later, scientists began to use the name *poliomyelitis*. This name comes from two Greek words. *Polios* means "gray," and *myelos* means "spinal cord." The words were put together to mean a disease of the gray matter in the spinal cord. This gray matter is soft tissue made up of nerves within the bony sections of the spinal column.

In 1835, an English physician had written about some small children with polio. During the 1800s, in the United States, several outbreaks of polio were described by physicians. But the epidemic of 1916 was the first widespread polio epidemic in this country. Polio epidemics have taken place at different times in countries all over the world, including Denmark, Sweden, France, Germany, Belgium, India, Singapore, Japan, Korea, and the Philippines.

Not all cases of polio are the same. Polio can be very mild and pass away quietly. In fact, most people who are infected with polio get well without developing any paralysis. While they are sick, they may suffer from headache, fever, sore throat, vomiting, and diarrhea. Many other diseases have these same symptoms (signs). It is often hard for physicians to tell that a patient has polio.

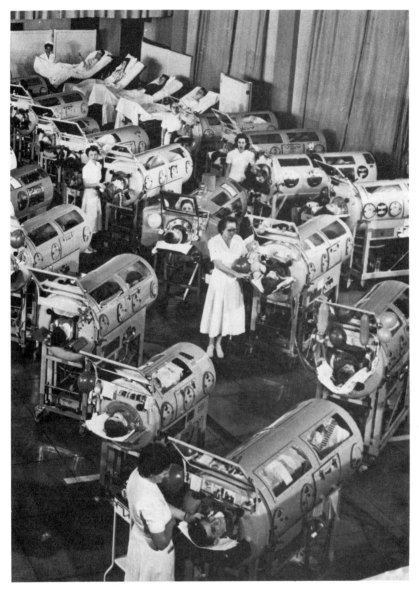

*When polio affected its victims' breathing, the patients were sometimes
placed in iron lungs.*

A serious case of polio is quite different. The patient develops pain in the back, arms, and legs. The neck may become stiff. Muscles feel tender. One man who lived through polio said it felt as if a dentist were drilling on the nerves all over his body.

Paralysis is frightening as well as painful. In humans, the central nervous system is made up of the brain and the spinal cord. The spinal cord runs up the back, protected by the backbone. Nerve fibers in the spinal cord carry messages to and from the brain. When the poliovirus reaches the central nervous system, it injures or destroys nerve cells. Then, when messages cannot reach muscles, the limbs (arms and legs) will not move.

While some patients lose the use of their arms or legs, others cannot move at all. A nurse told Richard Carter (the author of a book called *Breakthrough*) that she could never forget a teenager who lay in bed, completely paralyzed, and cried because he could not kill himself.

The most serious form of poliovirus attacks nerve cells in the brain that control breathing. The patient cannot breathe without the help of a machine such as an "iron lung," developed in the 1930s. Iron lungs were large machines; today, modern respirators or ventilators are used. Polio can also affect swallowing and talking.

It is difficult for physicians to say what will happen to a particular patient. Some polio patients die. Others must wear braces and walk with the help of canes and crutches. Still others can only get around in wheelchairs.

Paralytic polio changes a person's whole life—and the lives of family and friends. The care of a paralyzed patient is expensive. It is also time-consuming and emotionally difficult. Everyone has to face the fact that the patient may never be cured. Much of the damage from polio never goes away.

2

The Man Who Overcame Polio

In 1918, when Jonas was four years old, another epidemic took place in the United States—and in many other countries. This time, it was an epidemic of influenza, or "flu." Just as World War I was coming to a close, the flu struck. It killed more than 22 million of the world's people, twice as many as had died in fighting the war. A half million Americans died from it, many of them soldiers. Doctors were at a loss to know what to do to help the sick or stop the flu from spreading. Again, a mysterious killer had shown people how far they had to go in conquering contagious (catching) diseases. Contagious diseases are those that can be passed from one person to another.

Three years later, an important man came down with polio. In the years that followed, this man's illness affected the lives of thousands of people, including Jonas Salk.

Franklin Delano Roosevelt was thirty-nine years old in 1921. He was wealthy, good-looking, well educated, and from a well-known and influential family. Franklin was well liked by almost everyone who met him. He was a lawyer and politician. He had held several government offices. In 1920, he had run unsuccessfully for vice president of the United States. His cousin Theodore Roosevelt had been president, and many of his friends believed Franklin would also become president one day.

Franklin, some friends, his wife, Eleanor, and their five small children were all on vacation at their summer home when he fell ill. Their house was on Canada's Campobello Island, off the coast of northern Maine. One evening in August, after a day of boating and swimming, Roosevelt sat down to go through his mail. He was still wearing his wet bathing suit. Soon he began to shiver. Instead of eating supper, he went to bed and tried to get warm.

By morning he was in great pain and running a high temperature. A physician came, but he could not tell what was wrong. Steadily, the pain became worse. Then Roosevelt's legs, back, arms, and hands became paralyzed. He could not move. A second physician arrived. He guessed that Franklin had a blood clot in his lower back.

The physician suggested that Franklin's muscles should be massaged (rubbed). Although this was so painful the sick man could hardly bear it, it seemed to bring life back into his hands. His wife, Eleanor, and his best friend, Louis Howe, stayed with him night and day.

Days passed, then weeks, but Franklin still had a fever, and he was still in pain all of the time. Finally, physicians realized that he had a "children's disease," infantile paralysis.

Everyone was afraid the Roosevelt children would also come down with polio, but they did not. Neither did Eleanor nor any of the other people around Franklin at Campobello.

In the middle of September, Roosevelt was moved to

Presbyterian Hospital in New York City. Because he was so well known, he was put on a train in secrecy, so strangers would not see how sick he was. Already, he was determined never to complain and never to let himself become discouraged. At Presbyterian Hospital he struggled to rebuild his strength by pulling himself up on the rings that hung over his bed. Eleanor backed him all the way. His plan was to go right on with the busy life he had lived before his illness.

Before he went home from the hospital at the end of October, Roosevelt could sit up with pillows behind his back. He was able to use his arms and shoulders. But it would be a long time before he could stand again. And then he could only stand with the help of crutches and forty pounds of steel braces on his legs. Most of the time, he moved around his house in a wheelchair.

Swimming was one activity Franklin enjoyed. The water supported his helpless legs. His physicians agreed that this form of exercise was good for him.

Roosevelt kept up his political activities, mostly by mail. He exercised. He swam. He practiced using crutches at home. Near the end of 1922, more than a year after he had first come down with polio, he returned to his office at an insurance company in New York City. Entering the building on the first day, he fell when one of his crutches slipped on the floor. A young man hurried over to help him. This man, Basil O'Connor, was a lawyer who worked in the same building. Soon he and Roosevelt became friends.

At the 1924 Democratic National Convention in New York, Franklin Roosevelt made an important speech nominating Alfred E. Smith for president. A great crowd of people packed Madison Square Garden to hear him. He came onto the platform in his wheelchair. But when it was time to speak, he stood—with some help—prepared his crutches, and moved to the speaker's desk on his own. While he spoke, he braced himself against the desk. Smith did not win the nomination. But newspaper writers called Roosevelt "the real hero of the Democratic Convention." Everyone saw that he was a born leader, with or without the use of his legs.

Shortly after the convention, Roosevelt took a trip to Warm Springs, a small town in Georgia. It is about seventy-five miles south of Atlanta. He went to see a natural pool of mineral water that was always warm. He stayed in a small cottage near the Meriwether Inn, an old hotel that was not in very good condition. Roosevelt had heard about the run-down resort from its owner.

In Warm Springs he met Louis Joseph, who had been paralyzed by polio. Thanks to the warm water of the spring, Joseph could now walk using only canes.

As soon as Roosevelt entered the warm pool, he grew excited about the possibilities. He knew that swimming had helped him before. Because the water was warm, he could stay in the pool as long as he wanted. He hoped this beautiful, sunny place would help him recover the strength in his legs. He exercised in the water as often as possible. Sure enough, a few days later he was able to stand in the water and even take a few steps.

The old resort at Warm Springs, Georgia, became very important to Franklin Roosevelt. He told many people about it after he returned to New York. He believed he had found a place that might be helpful to others who had been crippled. Newspaper articles about Warm Springs began to appear, because Roosevelt was in the news and his activities were news. Soon, sick people began traveling to Georgia, hoping they would get better there. So many came that some of the other vacationers staying in the old Meriwether Inn objected.

They were afraid they might catch polio from the recovering polio patients.

With his own money, Roosevelt had another pool built just for crippled people. A new dining room just for them was added to the inn. Roosevelt went on working, building up his muscles with the help of doctors at home and in Georgia. The next summer he could walk on crutches with only one brace on his left leg. His right leg had grown stronger.

The resort at Warm Springs was not very successful for its owner. So Roosevelt bought it. He wanted to turn it into a rehabilitation center, a place where polio patients and others could work on their injured bodies. Roosevelt and his friend, Basil O'Connor, had formed a law partnership. When O'Connor saw Warm Springs, he was not as hopeful as Roosevelt. Still, in 1926, he helped Roosevelt start a non-profit corporation called the Warm Springs Foundation. Soon physicians came to work for the foundation at Warm Springs. Plans were made to improve the buildings and grounds. Roosevelt and his friends—some of them very wealthy men—became the officers of the new corporation. Basil O'Connor was made secretary-treasurer.

In 1927, Roosevelt stayed at Warm Springs for several months. He had his own cottage there. He was strong enough to stand on the ground, between parallel bars, for several minutes *with both hands raised.* No wonder he delighted in Warm Springs and all he had accomplished there.

Of course, Roosevelt had never even thought about giving up his career in politics. In 1928, he ran for governor of New York State, and when he won, he turned Warm Springs over to his partner. The job of keeping Warm Springs going was quite a challenge. O'Connor found he enjoyed it much more than he had expected. But it was not long before the Warm Springs Foundation was seriously short of funds. After the 1929 stock market crash, its rich backers had little money left to give to charity.

In 1932, Roosevelt was elected president of the United States. He had regained the use of many of his muscles. Only his lower legs and his knees had to be supported by braces. He was always careful not to appear handicapped in front of the public.

Now when President Roosevelt went to Georgia, many of his associates went along. A larger house, called the Little White House, had been built for him at Warm Springs. Still, O'Connor needed help. The rehabilitation center could not keep going much longer without money to pay the bills.

A public relations expert named Carl Byoir had an idea. He thought ordinary people, not just rich people, would pay to go to a dance in honor of their president's birthday. Roosevelt's first birthday as president of the United States was his fifty-second birthday. On January 30, 1934, Birthday Balls were held in his honor. The main aim was to raise money for the Warm Springs Foundation. More than 6,000 birthday dances were held all over the country. During the party in Washington, D.C., Roosevelt spoke over the radio. He told how handicapped people like him were being helped at Warm Springs, especially people who had suffered from polio. He ended by describing this as "the happiest birthday I ever have known." After expenses had been paid, the Warm Springs Foundation received $1,016,443 as a result of the president's Birthday Balls of 1934.

In the years that followed, birthday dances were held again, but less money was raised each year. In 1936, Roosevelt was elected president for a second term. He was still very popular, although he had more critics of his policies every year. Some people did not think he should be using his office to raise money, even if the cause was a worthy one.

In the fall of 1937, Roosevelt and O'Connor set up a new foundation, the National Foundation for Infantile Paralysis (NFIP). Its purpose was to fight polio in every way possible. The National Foundation would search for ways of preventing polio. It would also raise money to treat the disease and to help patients recover and start living normal lives again. The rehabilitation center at Warm Springs would be just one of many centers in the United States.

The new National Foundation was incorporated on January 3, 1938. Basil O'Connor was its president. His friendship with Franklin Roosevelt had certainly given a new direction to O'Connor's life. Now he was involved full-time in the fight against polio.

That year there were no Birthday Balls. O'Connor knew Americans still wanted to do something about polio, but because of the depression they had little money. Perhaps the average person felt his or her small contribution would not count for much. At this point, a famous entertainer, Eddie Cantor, suggested that the foundation sponsor a radio appeal for money. All the national radio programs from Hollywood, California, were asked to give thirty seconds of broadcast time. Cantor had the perfect name for the appeal. He wanted to call it the March of Dimes.

This little phrase was magic. People loved it. Cantor's new slogan made a small contribution—just a dime—seem important. Local chapters of the National Foundation for Infantile Paralysis were starting up in American cities. Members worked hard to make the March of Dimes a success.

The campaign began on Roosevelt's birthday with the short radio appeal. People were asked to send their dimes to

President Franklin D. Roosevelt and Basil O'Connor (right) at a news conference in the White House. They thanked Americans for their contributions to the March of Dimes.

the White House in Washington, D.C.

For two days, workers at the White House were afraid the appeal had failed. Less than twenty dollars had come in. But the next morning's mail was unbelievable! No one could find the official White House mail because 30,000 letters had been delivered. After two more days the total had risen to 230,000 letters. People sent dimes wrapped in tape—even dimes inside cakes. The National Foundation was off to a wonderful start. Through its first campaign it raised $1,823,045. And every year, O'Connor and his army of enthusiastic workers held a new campaign. There had never been anything quite like it before. The National Foundation went on to raise more money for polio than had ever been raised to overcome any other disease.

A lot of this money was given to scientists who were studying polio and other diseases caused by viruses. Franklin Roosevelt, the president who walked with crutches, made the March of Dimes possible. The March of Dimes would later make it possible for Jonas Salk to become a polio fighter.

3

There Is More in Life Than Money

Science was not emphasized at Townsend Harris High School. While he was in high school, Jonas Salk took only one science course, physics. He only took physics because his friends were taking it. He had fully expected to become a lawyer. One of his greatest interests was literature. All his life he enjoyed quoting lines from the works of such great writers as Ralph Waldo Emerson, Henry David Thoreau, Roger Bacon, and Abraham Lincoln.

Jonas was a slender, dark-haired teenager. He was too small for sports, but he loved music and he liked to dance. Music was another interest he kept up after he finished school. He always liked to go to classical concerts when he could take time away from his work.

As a teenager, Jonas spent some of his summers working in the mountains north of New York City. He worked as a counselor in a boys' camp. He was well liked by his schoolmates and by the younger boys he directed in the summer.

In his first year at the City College of New York, Jonas signed up for some science courses simply to try something different. He was surprised that he enjoyed them so much. He soon changed his goal and began to aim for medical school instead of law school.

While he was in college, Jonas earned his own way. His parents took out a loan to help him start medical school. But after that he paid for his own education. He earned scholarships and took whatever part-time jobs came his way.

Most of the other students at the New York University School of Medicine, where Salk studied after he had graduated from City College, enjoyed learning to diagnose, that is, to identify, different diseases and to treat them. Salk, however, became more and more interested in the work of research scientists, people who spend their lives doing medical research in the laboratory.

Salk certainly could have become a medical doctor at a hospital or even a physician with his own private practice. This was his mother's dream—for Jonas to open an office in New York City. But he was not as interested in practicing medicine as he was in working in a laboratory.

Perhaps the only thing really unusual about this was that Jonas was turning his back on a way of making a good living. In the Great Depression of the 1930s, finding a way to make a living and support a family was foremost in the minds of most men. But sometime during his years in school, scientific research came to mean more to Jonas than either his early dream of becoming a lawyer or his later dream of a medical career.

A life of searching for scientific answers and working on carefully planned experiments seemed ideal to the young student. When he applied for admission to the New York University School of Medicine, an interviewer warned him that he would not get rich in the field of research. "There is more in life than money," Salk answered.

At the end of his freshman year in medical school, one of his teachers helped Salk get an important fellowship. Fellowships are usually sums of money given to excellent students to encourage their studies beyond the four-year college level. This made it possible for him to take a year off. He spent that year learning all about biochemistry, the study of the chemicals and chemical processes of living things. Then, after he was back in medical school, his teachers began to see that Salk was different from his fellow students. He was turning into a skilled laboratory worker with ideas of his own.

As if he did not have enough work to do, Salk also joined a special group of students. These students sat in during weekly discussions held by some of their teachers. Salk went to these meetings every week, although he did not earn extra credit for doing so. In his third year at medical school, he was elected to Alpha Omega Alpha, an important society honoring high achievers.

In his last year, Salk and some other seniors were given a new opportunity. They could choose to do something different from their regular class work for a period of two months. Salk had become excited about the field of bacteriology, the science that deals with the tiny life-forms called bacteria. He chose to work with Dr. Thomas Francis, Jr.

Francis was the chief teacher of bacteriology at the New York University School of Medicine. He was a top microbiologist. (Microbiologists are scientists who study very tiny living things.) Francis was known for discovering one particular type of influenza virus. Viruses are very tiny protein substances that are able to grow and multiply only in living cells. Some viruses, such as the flu virus, cause diseases. Salk knew it was an honor to spend his two months working with Dr. Thomas Francis, Jr.

As it happened, Francis was one of the few microbiologists interested in the possibilities of killed-virus vaccines. A vaccine is material that stimulates the body's immune system to produce antibodies against a particular disease. These antibodies then protect the person if he or she gets infected by the actual disease-causing organism. Such a protected person is then said to be immune to the disease. Vaccines have to be powerful enough to get the body to produce antibodies, but not so strong as to cause the actual disease.

When Salk started to work with Francis, he was looking into the idea that a special treatment with ultraviolet irradiation could make flu viruses harmless. These killed-viruses might then be used in a vaccine. This treatment would not stop the viruses from giving a person immunity. At least, that was what Francis hoped to prove in his experiments.

Francis especially liked the knowledge Salk had gained during his year spent studying biochemistry. Salk was helpful to Francis because he really understood the influenza virus experiments. Part of Salk's job was taking out the lungs of mice that had influenza. Then he removed the virus from the mouse lungs. These experiences were the beginning of Salk's work with infectious viruses.

During his senior year, Salk dated a young woman named Donna Lindsay. Donna was a graduate of Smith College. She had chosen a career in social welfare work, and she was a student at the New York School of Social Work. Her family was richer than Salk's family—her father was a dentist—but the two young Jews had many of the same interests. They both wanted to help others. Donna found that Jonas was easy to talk to and he had something to say about a lot of subjects, not just science. Then, too, they both loved music and dancing. Jonas and Donna were married on the day after Jonas graduated from medical school in 1939.

After receiving his medical degree, Jonas—now Jonas Salk, M.D.—went on working in the laboratory with Dr. Francis. He received a grant of a hundred dollars a month from the Rockefeller Foundation. This gift helped him to go on working in science. Grants from private groups and foundations or from the government often are the main means of support for laboratory scientists.

In March 1940, Dr. Salk became an intern at Mount Sinai Hospital in New York City. Interns are new doctors who are learning to work with patients—and with other physicians. Salk had won a place for himself that very few people could hope to win. That year 250 top medical students from all around the country wanted to be interns at Mount Sinai. Only 12 were selected.

Salk worked as an intern at the famous hospital for two years. He succeeded because he was calm, a hard worker, and a person who could get along with others. While he was serving his internship at Mount Sinai, Salk was elected by his fellow physicians to the position of president of the house staff. This was something like the position of class president at school. In dealings with hospital administrators, Salk was a spokesperson for all the doctors working on the Mount Sinai staff.

As a physician, Salk was especially good at diagnosis— that is, identifying diseases by their signs and symptoms. His surgical skills were excellent, too. Still, Salk's heart was in the laboratory, as it had been for some time now. He remained in close touch with Francis. He kept thinking about his special interest: how the body can gain immunity to a disease caused by a virus. Scientists of the day did not know very much about viruses. Virology was still a young field. Researchers were more experienced in working with bacteria. It was slow going, trying to unlock the secrets of viruses.

Once again war clouds had formed over Europe. Americans were watching Hitler's moves, fearful of what the future might bring. Nazi Germany had invaded Poland in 1939 and had taken over France in 1940. Britain and the Soviet Union and other countries were fighting against Germany. World War II had begun in Europe. Was it possible that the United States would get involved in this war as it had in World War I? The answer came in late 1941. Japan, Germany's ally, attacked U.S. forces in Hawaii. The United States then entered the war against Germany and Japan.

Toward the end of his internship, Salk began to think that his future must lie in research. Mount Sinai was known for refusing to keep its own interns as regular physicians. When the time came, the hospital would not give Salk a job on its staff. Salk thought he might become a resident physician at the hospital of the Rockefeller Institute. He had worked with scientists there as part of his work with Francis. But he was refused again.

No one could have had a better school record. No one could have been better liked by his co-workers. Salk was very disappointed.

When he failed to find a job as a physician in his hometown, Salk turned again to Francis. His teacher now was at the University of Michigan at Ann Arbor. He was the head of the Department of Epidemiology in Michigan's new School of Public Health. Epidemiology is the medical science that deals with the location, spread, and control of diseases in a population. Francis was still working on influenza vaccines. He also had been given grants that were to be used for studies of polio epidemics. These grants came from the

National Foundation for Infantile Paralysis (NFIP), the organization set up by Franklin D. Roosevelt and Basil O'Connor a few years earlier.

Salk planned to get a fellowship and gain some more experience with viruses. Then he would go to Ann Arbor and work with Francis.

But the United States had entered World War II at just this time. Francis's studies of the influenza virus became the most important work to be done. The U.S. Army wanted scientists to develop a vaccine against flu as quickly as possible. Everyone wanted to prevent another outbreak of flu like the one in 1918 that had killed so many soldiers. So, as it turned out, Salk spent no more time preparing for his career. He hurried off to the University of Michigan to work with Francis. He would receive about forty dollars a week for one year, provided in part by a grant from the National Foundation.

The Salks lived in a rented farmhouse on the edge of the university town of Ann Arbor. They were both busy. Donna had a job as a social worker with the Family and Children's Service, and of course, Jonas was in the laboratory. But they were able to enjoy their new home in the country together. They went for long walks. Jonas planted a large garden, and Donna learned to can—to pack and preserve—vegetables. Everything, especially their wood-burning stove, was new and exciting to these "city kids." While they were living in Ann Arbor, the Salks had two sons. Peter was born in 1944, and Darrell was born in 1947.

Money from the National Foundation helped support Salk and his growing family, but he worked on influenza, not polio. Francis was delighted to have him. He knew that Salk was willing to take hold and not just wait to be told what to do next. Francis was doing studies of epidemics for the

National Foundation. He was also the head of a U.S. Army group that was later called the Armed Forces Epidemiological Board. There was no time to waste in Francis's laboratory, and he felt that Salk fit right in. Salk did not become a soldier. He was given a draft deferment because he was doing important work for the government.

With Salk's help, Francis did develop a successful influenza vaccine. The army used it on millions of American soldiers in the 1940s. Salk's experiments at Ann Arbor helped Francis prove that there was a relationship between the amount of antibody in the blood and a person's immunity to a disease caused by a virus. More antibodies meant greater protection. Francis and Salk were also able to show that a vaccine made from killed virus started the production of antibodies in the blood just as did a case of influenza— that is, infection with the strong live virus. In other words, the virus could be killed with Formalin, a solution of the chemical formaldehyde. And if then given as a vaccine, the killed virus could still trigger the body to produce antibodies.

Francis had been working with attenuated (weakened but living) flu viruses for a long time. But the army could not take the chance that a live virus might suddenly return to full strength. A live-virus vaccine might kill people. So the safer, yet just as powerful, killed-virus vaccine won out.

What did Salk do in his daily work as a scientist? One example of his work is a method he developed for finding out how much influenza antibody was in a particular sample of blood. He also acted as director of the Army Influenza Commission when Francis could not be there. Once Salk traveled to an army base where soldiers had an unusual form of pneumonia. Salk found that it was really flu. It was, in fact, a type of flu virus that was not in the vaccine they were getting ready to test. Fortunately, Salk saw to it that this form of the flu virus was part of the final vaccine.

Slightly different forms of the same kind of virus are called *types*. And different forms of the same type of virus are called *strains*. One type of virus can include many different strains. Salk and Francis learned that the more strains of virus that are included in a vaccine, the more useful the vaccine will be. This is because such a vaccine gets the body to produce more kinds of antibodies to fight more varieties of the disease.

During the winter of 1943–44, Francis tested his flu vaccine "in the field." That is, he gave it to more than two thousand students in the Army Specialized Training Program. Half the students were given the real vaccine. The other half were given a *placebo*, an inactive substance that could neither help nor harm them. No one knew which students had received the real vaccine. The results were carefully watched, and good records were kept. When the test was over, the group of students who had really been vaccinated had 75 percent fewer cases of flu than did the control group. (The control group was the group of students who received the harmless placebo.)

Another important thing happened. The students who had received the vaccine did not become ill. Therefore, they did not spread the flu virus to the other students. As a result, even students who had not taken part in Francis's test escaped the flu that winter. Epidemiologists call this result of a vaccination program the *herd effect*. It happens every time a large number of people are vaccinated against a disease. When people living in a certain place are vaccinated, that sickness does not spread as widely as it would ordinarily have spread. Many of the people who were not vaccinated will still stay free of the disease since there are fewer sick people to catch it from.

Francis was the head of the laboratory at Ann Arbor. But he shared his successes with the others who worked with him. This was good for Salk and good of Francis. When articles about their work were printed in scientific journals, Francis would use Salk's name as well as his own. Salk was not bashful about it. He sometimes asked Francis to list his name first. Salk still felt as sure of himself as he had felt back in high school. He was proud of his abilities. He wanted to get credit for the work he was doing, and he wanted to do more independent work.

Salk had entered his thirties. He thought that his way of working—studying viruses with emphasis on immunology— was unusual and valuable. (Immunology is the study of the body's defenses against disease.) Salk began to dream of having more freedom than he had at the University of Michigan. He thought that he could contribute more than some other virologists—experts on viruses—because of his special point of view.

At the end of World War II in 1945, Salk did some more traveling for the U.S. government. This time he went to Germany to set up some new laboratories for the study of influenza. Flu epidemics were expected there. This work was pleasing to Salk. He was honored to have been chosen. He also enjoyed the chance to organize and plan things his own way.

In 1946, Salk was made an assistant professor in the Department of Epidemiology at the University of Michigan at Ann Arbor. But he was restless. He really wanted to move on to a job where he could set up his own laboratory.

4

Germs, Viruses, and Vaccines

From the day he decided to become a medical researcher, Jonas Salk's life was his work. His work took place in the laboratory where he studied bacteria, viruses, and vaccines.

Some researchers study their subjects in order to add to the sum of human knowledge. Others work to create new products that will make daily life easier. Still others look for the answers to problems such as disease. Salk was one of these. When he studied viruses, he studied them from the point of view of an immunologist. That is, he did not study viruses just to learn more about them. He was looking for ways to help the body fight off viruses that cause disease.

The story of immunology began long before Salk entered his first laboratory. Some wise physicians in ancient Greece and Rome guessed that diseases were caused by something too small to be seen. But this mysterious some-thing was forgotten for a long time. For centuries, no one knew anything at all about germs. When people fell ill, physicians blamed "bad air" or evil spirits. Often, they decided the sick person had done something wrong and was being punished for it.

Three hundred years ago, people had no idea they were surrounded by tiny living creatures they could not see. Then curious people began to study small things through lenses. Lenses are pieces of glass shaped so they will bend light. The first microscopes were simple instruments with one lens. They made leaves, seeds, and insects look bigger. But they were not very well made and they did not give a sharp, clear picture.

In 1677, a Dutch shopkeeper made a wonderful discovery. Antonie van Leeuwenhoek looked through a little lens, which he had carefully shaped and polished. He saw tiny creatures moving around in a drop of pond water. These microorganisms delighted Leeuwenhoek. But he did not imagine that they could be dangerous. He just went on making better lenses and discovering smaller creatures. The smallest creatures Leeuwenhoek saw looked like fuzzy dots under his microscope. Today, we know they were bacteria. Bacteria are what most people are talking about when they use the word *germs*.

One hundred and fifty years went by. Then Joseph Jackson Lister, an English lens maker, made a much better microscope. Lister's 1830 microscope made tiny things look larger—and also sharp and clear.

A German botanist (a scientist who studies plants) named Ferdinand Julius Cohn used the new microscope in his laboratory. He discovered many things, including the microscopic plants we call *algae*.

In the 1860s, Cohn turned his attention to bacteria. He learned a lot about how bacteria looked, acted, and multiplied. He classified them, too, and wrote an important book about them. Cohn became the world's first bacteriologist.

While scientists like Cohn were watching and describing bacteria, others were trying to solve the mysteries of illness. They wondered, for example, why some patients died of the disease called *smallpox* and others lived through it. They wondered why the patients who lived never had smallpox again.

Some people believed healthy children should be "given" smallpox on purpose. Smallpox caused painful blisters to break out on the skin. If someone stuck a needle into a smallpox blister and then scratched a healthy person's skin, that person might have a mild case of smallpox. Then he or she would be safe and could never catch the disease again. But often the experiment failed and the healthy person died. Though some were desperate enough to try this experiment, smallpox was a terrible disease on which to take a chance.

An Englishman, Edward Jenner, was the first physician to truly vaccinate a person against a disease. The disease was smallpox. When Jenner was working in the country, he noticed that farm people sometimes caught a disease known as *cowpox* from their animals. Cowpox was something like smallpox, but its victims only had a few blisters and then got well. They hardly knew they had been sick at all. The farmers told Jenner that if you had cowpox you would never catch smallpox. Unlike other physicians, Edward Jenner thought a lot about this strange "old wives' tale."

Jenner worked on the problem of immunity to smallpox for twenty years. Then he carried out a very dangerous experiment. In 1796 he pricked a blister on the hand of a woman who had cowpox. Then he scratched the skin of a healthy young boy with the same needle. Sure enough, the boy became sick. A cowpox blister appeared right on the spot where Jenner's needle had broken the skin.

Two months later, Jenner wanted to see if the boy really had become immune to smallpox. He scratched the boy's arm again. This time the material on his needle came from a *smallpox* blister, but the boy did not get sick.

Although he did not know *why* his patient had become immune to smallpox, Jenner knew *how* to immunize people. He had invented vaccination. (*Vaccinia* is the scientific name for cowpox.) Everyone feared smallpox so much that Jenner's method of vaccination was soon in use in many parts of the world.

As it turned out, smallpox was the only disease that could be overcome this way—by giving people a milder case of a related disease. Still, scientists were encouraged to search for other ways of preventing diseases. Some of them were beginning to understand that small, invisible creatures might be causing illnesses. If these microorganisms could be stopped, so could the diseases.

Unbelievably, however, most physicians did not understand the connection between bacteria and disease. They wanted to go on working the same way they had always worked. In the 1840s, a Hungarian physician, Ignaz Semmelweis, thought otherwise. Semmelweis guessed that physicians themselves were passing diseases from sick patients to healthy patients. He worked in a maternity hospital. Many of the mothers of new babies became sick and died of childbed, or puerperal, fever in his hospital.

When he was put in charge, Semmelweis ordered all the physicians to change their habits. He made them wash their hands in strong chemicals before they worked on each patient. Fewer mothers caught childbed fever, but the other physicians became angry. They were insulted. And they would not believe something on their hands—something they could not see—was causing sickness. Semmelweis lost his job at the hospital.

In 1862, the great French chemist Louis Pasteur finally proved that diseases were caused by creatures too tiny to be seen without a microscope. Pasteur figured out that many diseases were contagious. They were being passed from one living being to another. Of course, this observation supported his "germ theory."

In 1867, an English surgeon named Joseph Lister succeeded where Semmelweis had failed. Lister taught physicians to clean their hands and their instruments and bandages with carbolic acid before touching patients. (This man was the son of Joseph Jackson Lister, the microscope maker.)

In 1881, Pasteur became the second scientist to stop a disease by vaccination. One disease he studied was anthrax, a disease that killed cattle and sheep. He had no cowpox to help him. But he had already found that heating would kill unwanted bacteria in wine. He hit upon the idea of heating bacteria taken from animals that were sick with anthrax. He did not kill the anthrax bacteria. He just weakened them so they could only grow very slowly. When he gave these specially treated bacteria (attenuated bacteria) to a healthy sheep, that animal became immune to anthrax. Pasteur understood that the animal's body had somehow developed the ability to kill the powerful anthrax germs.

Soon many scientists were working on the problem of disease-causing germs. Robert Koch, a German physician, founded the science of microbiology. He discovered a new way to grow bacteria in dishes of jelly in his laboratory. He was able to separate out each different kind of bacteria and study it. Koch discovered the bacteria that cause tuberculosis, cholera, and bubonic plague. And, like Pasteur, he learned to prepare vaccines by weakening the bacteria that he used.

In 1885, Pasteur again used weakened germs to fight a deadly disease. This time his patient was a boy who had been bitten by a "mad" dog, a dog with rabies. Up until then, rabies had always killed, but first it took about two weeks to reach an infected person's brain. Pasteur gave the boy injections (shots) of weakened rabies germs. He had developed this vaccine in the laboratory using the spinal cords of rabbits that had rabies. Every day, the boy received another injection of slightly stronger germs. He did not develop rabies, and he did not die.

But Pasteur had a special problem with rabies. Try as he might, he could not find the bacteria that caused it. Rabies was clearly a contagious disease. It could be passed from sick animals to healthy ones. Pasteur looked and looked through his microscope, but he could never find the rabies bacteria.

Dimitri Ivanovski, a Russian scientist, studied a disease that killed tobacco plants. He made a juice from the leaves of sick plants. He could not see any germs in this juice. But it would pass the disease along to healthy plants. Ivanovski used filters to try to find the missing germs. Even a filter with very small holes in it would not stop the germs. The juice that came through his filter still made healthy tobacco plants sick.

A Dutch scientist came up with a name for these tiny germs in 1898. Martinus Willem Beijerinck was studying the same tobacco plant disease. He couldn't see the germs either. But he knew they were there, and he named them *viruses*, using a Latin word meaning "a poisonous juice."

It was not until the 1930s that scientists using electron microscopes were able to see viruses. Pasteur, Ivanovski, and

Beijerinck had been on the right track. The viruses were there. They were just too small to be seen, even with a regular microscope.

An electron microscope uses a beam of electrons (electrically charged particles) instead of a beam of light to "see" things. On November 16, 1953, *Time* printed this news story.

In all the years that medical researchers have been studying poliomyelitis, they had never seen the critter. Now two teams have isolated the virus, looked at it long and hard under the electron microscope, photographed it, and measured it. It turns out to be a spherical particle almost exactly one millionth of an inch in diameter. Magnified tens of thousands of times against a plastic screen, the virus particles look like tennis balls on an asphalt court.

The reason for the long delay in completely isolating the virus was the difficulty of separating it from the substances in which it grows. Until recently, a relatively "pure" preparation was only 1% virus and 99% "gunk."

Bacteria are one-celled, living creatures. But a virus has no cell parts. It is just a piece of what is known as *nucleic acid*, with an outer coat of protein called the *capsid*.

A virus is a parasite. It only lives when it enters a living cell. Different viruses can live in plants, animals, and bacteria. Outside the body of its host, a virus is nothing but some chemicals.

When a virus enters a cell, it takes over. Using the cell's own tools for making proteins and reproducing nucleic acid (DNA, hereditary material), the virus causes the cell to make new viruses. When these new viruses break out, the cell dies. Then the viruses invade more cells.

Sometimes a virus remains inactive inside a host cell for

a long time. Then it suddenly reproduces itself. For example, people can have the AIDS virus for years before becoming sick.

What happens when a harmful virus or bacterium enters someone's body? Somehow, the body knows it is a foreign substance. Scientists call the invader an *antigen*. When an antigen appears, the body begins to produce *antibodies*. Antibodies are special proteins. They provide protection against antigens.

Each kind of antibody fits one particular antigen; they fit like a lock and key. Once an antibody combines with an

The poliovirus as seen through an electronic microscope.

antigen, disease-fighting white blood cells can swallow the "foreigner" and destroy it.

The immune system is the system inside our bodies that helps them fight off diseases. Newborn babies for a time have natural immunity obtained from their mothers. They are safe from many diseases. Growing children can become immune to other diseases, too. For example, children who catch mumps and measles become immune to them. They will never have these diseases a second time. Their bodies go on making antibodies against mumps and measles as long as they live.

Vaccines give the body another kind of immunity. A vaccine causes the body to make antibodies against a disease. A vaccine for measles does not make a person sick with measles. But it makes that person's body produce antibodies against the measles virus. Then, if the measles virus really attacks, the vaccinated person can fight it off just as if he or she had already had the disease.

No one knows exactly what makes vaccines "work." In the case of some viruses, the capsid, or outer coat, may be the antigen that triggers the production of antibodies.

Antibiotics such as penicillin and streptomycin, which were developed in the 1940s, are substances that will kill bacteria. But a virus cannot be killed by antibiotics or most other drugs. That is one reason why vaccines are so important. They can prevent diseases caused by viruses.

5

Steps Forward, Steps Back

In 1908, in Vienna, two scientists named Karl Landsteiner and Erwin Popper gave polio to monkeys. They used tissue from the spine of a human who had died from polio. They knew the disease was caused by a dangerous virus. Now they had a laboratory animal they could use in studying that virus.

The next year, two Americans, Simon Flexner and P. A. Lewis of the Rockefeller Institute of Medical Research, showed that the disease could be passed from one monkey to another.

Both Landsteiner and Flexner learned that monkeys that had had polio would not get it again. They thought it would be possible, perhaps, to use a vaccine to stop polio.

But no one knew enough about the disease, or about viruses, to develop a vaccine at that time. Also, people hoped they would find another way to prevent polio. Maybe cleanliness or better nutrition was the answer. Maybe they would discover that an animal such as the rat was giving polio to people.

In 1935, the Birthday Ball Commission began giving grants of money to scientists who would study polio. We know now that poliovirus enters a person's mouth and grows in the intestines—part of the digestive system. Then, in serious cases, the virus travels to the spinal cord or the brain. This was not known in 1935. In fact, very little was known about the disease.

Monkeys were costly, hard to get, and harder to keep. No one had any idea that the poliovirus could be found in the bloodstream of a sick person. Scientists thought it passed directly from the nose to the brain. Most of them decided it would be of little use to try to develop a vaccine. Monkeys that had had polio and lived did not seem to have a lot of antibodies in their blood. The scientists did not guess what was wrong with this observation. Their problem was that they simply lacked the tools they needed to measure the true number of viruses and antibodies in monkey blood and human blood.

Strangely enough, in 1935, two vaccines against polio were not only developed but also tested on children.

Maurice Brodie, a young researcher, made a polio vaccine. He ground up the spinal cords of monkeys that had polio. Then he added a chemical (formaldehyde) to kill the virus. He took some of the vaccine himself, and he did not get sick.

Brodie had the backing of an important man, Dr. William H. Park. Park was director of the Bureau of Laboratories of the New York City Department of Health. Because Dr. Park was a well-known scientist, Brodie's work was not questioned as it should have been. His vaccine was given to 9,000 children.

After the test, some other scientists experimented with Brodie's vaccine. They gave it to monkeys. The monkeys lived, but when they were given living poliovirus, they died. The scientists decided that Brodie's vaccine might not kill children. But it also would not protect them against polio.

In the same year, Dr. John A. Kolmer of Temple University in Philadelphia prepared another vaccine. He did not use a killed-virus vaccine. Instead, he only weakened the poliovirus. He believed his vaccine would make children immune without giving them a case of polio. Kolmer tested his vaccine on 12,000 children. Three of the children were paralyzed by polio, and six children died.

Although the Brodie and Kolmer experiments were stopped, people, especially scientists, were troubled by the two failures.

When the National Foundation for Infantile Paralysis began to give out research grants, Dr. Thomas M. Rivers became Basil O'Connor's adviser. Rivers was an expert virologist. He had trained many young scientists while head of the hospital of the Rockefeller Institute of Medical Research. Rivers helped O'Connor by working out some questions that needed answers. What did polio do to the human body? How did it get into the body? How did it travel from one person to another? Where did the disease grow in the body? How did it reach the spinal cord and the brain? What was the best way to study the virus? Were there other laboratory animals that could be used instead of monkeys?

When the National Foundation began its work, scientists were trying to learn as much about polio as they could. They were *not* very interested in finding a way to prevent it by vaccination. They could not forget Brodie and Kolmer.

Basil O'Connor was not a scientist, but he was eager to learn along with the people who were given grants by his foundation. Men like Rivers enjoyed working with O'Connor because he did not try to tell researchers what to do. He did not even try to hurry them along. Instead, he accepted the fact that the fight against polio might be a long one.

During World War II, from 1940 to 1945, the National Foundation went on raising money. These funds were used to help polio patients and to pay for the training of scientists who would specialize in virology. Serious epidemics of polio struck the nation in 1943 and 1944. The public was worried about the war. American soldiers were fighting in Europe and Asia. But people did not forget the battle going on in laboratories at home. In 1945, the National Foundation for Infantile Paralysis collected more than $18 million.

In the mid-1940s, O'Connor began to think that many polio researchers were not doing anything new. They seemed to be repeating the same experiments others had already worked on. O'Connor believed the battle against polio could be won. When the war was over, he planned to lead his fund-raisers and scientists to victory.

In 1947, Salk left Ann Arbor and moved his family to Pittsburgh, Pennsylvania. He was thirty-three years old. Although the University of Pittsburgh School of Medicine was not known as a center for research, Jonas Salk saw great possibilities there. Dr. William S. McEllroy, dean of the medical school, saw great possibilities in Salk. He was delighted to be hiring one of the scientists who had developed the influenza vaccine. Other schools were receiving grants for their research programs, and Pittsburgh really needed to develop a program of its own. In short, McEllroy believed Salk would be a fine addition to the school of medicine.

Salk visited Pittsburgh and thought it was an ideal place for his work. Pittsburgh was a large steel-making city with environmental problems. However, its leaders had the money and the desire to clean up the sooty air and make it a more pleasant place to live. Salk found that the city hospital right next to the medical school had room to spare. He was told he could set up his new virus research laboratory there.

McEllroy promised to give him all the help he needed. His old friends, including Francis, thought Salk was making a mistake, but after more than five years of working under Francis in Michigan, he wanted to strike out on his own. Pittsburgh gave him that chance.

Salk was disappointed when his first quarters in Pittsburgh turned out to be small. He had to work in the basement of the old Municipal Hospital. Although in time he was able to gain more space, he discovered that he still could not work entirely on his own. He was the associate professor of bacteriology and pathology, but he had to work under another teacher. This was Dr. Max A. Lauffer, who had run the university's virus research program for years. Lauffer was an expert in plant viruses, not animal viruses. He and Salk did not share the same interests at all. In addition, Salk was something new at the medical school in Pittsburgh. Most of the other physician-teachers had offices and patients of their own. People at the school were not used to a full-time researcher.

Salk went on with his work on flu viruses under a grant from the Armed Forces Epidemiological Board. He made a place in his laboratory for lab animals and set to work on a vaccine with an adjuvant in it. The adjuvant was mostly mineral oil. It could make the flu vaccine more powerful. More strains of influenza virus could be included in a single shot when the adjuvant was used.

Then a man visited Pittsburgh, a man who was going to change Salk's life. Harry M. Weaver had been a professor of anatomy. Toward the end of 1947, Weaver came to Pittsburgh to talk to Dr. Salk, Dean McEllroy, and others. He had been hired by Basil O'Connor as the foundation's director of research. His job was to get to know all the different scientists working on polio. Weaver was trying to find out how the National Foundation scientists could work together. O'Connor wanted to see some results before people became discouraged and stopped sending money to the March of Dimes.

Weaver knew that many researchers would not take kindly to the idea of being "directed" by anyone. But he was a very intelligent man who knew just how to encourage scientists without stepping on their toes. With his assistant, Dr. Theodore E. Boyd, he traveled around the country. They stopped in at the laboratories of foundation grantees. The grantees were researchers whose work was supported by the National Foundation.

Weaver and Boyd talked to virologists in their own language. Of course, even before they arrived, scientists were interested in getting to know Weaver. As a leader in the National Foundation, he might, if he liked their work, be able to help them keep their experiments going.

At this time, many virologists still believed that vaccination against polio was impossible. They remembered all too well the early vaccines of Maurice Brodie and John Kolmer. Also, they held to the belief that the poliovirus would grow only in nervous tissue from the central nervous system. How could a vaccine made from the spinal cords of animals be given to children? An allergic reaction to the vaccine might take place in the brain. Material from the spinal cord just was not safe.

But every summer the polio season left hundreds of Americans with shrunken, useless limbs. Penicillin, sulfa drugs, and other medicines were being used to treat bacterial diseases. But they were no use in fighting the poliovirus.

Harry Weaver believed the prevention of polio was the way to go with research. He and other scientists were interested in the possibility that the poliovirus could grow in human intestines. The intestines are nonnervous tissue. They are *not* part of the central nervous system. Virus that was grown in a tissue different from the spinal cord could be used to make a safe vaccine. Perhaps polio was an intestinal infection, after all.

In March 1948, Dr. John F. Enders, a foundation grantee, was working at Harvard University in Massachusetts with two men named Thomas H. Weller and Frederick C. Robbins. They were experimenting with chicken-pox viruses. And they were using nonnervous tissue from human embryos (unborn and undeveloped babies). Almost by accident, they successfully grew poliovirus in flasks of nonnervous tissue!

Like many other scientific truths that are discovered almost by chance, this was a true breakthrough. It meant that polio researchers could now grow all the poliovirus they needed. It also made it possible for scientists to work toward a safe vaccine, free of nervous tissue. (For their achievement, Enders, Weller, and Robbins later won the Nobel Prize in physiology and medicine in 1954.)

Back in 1935, at the Rockefeller Institute, virologists Albert Sabin and Peter Olitsky had tried to grow poliovirus in nonnervous tissue. They felt they had proved that it could not be done. Then, after Enders and his associates did grow poliovirus in nonnervous tissue, Sabin looked at his old experiment again. He discovered that the particular virus he had used was the *only* poliovirus that would *not* grow in nonnervous tissue. What bad luck! Scientists might have started work on a vaccine much earlier. But Sabin and Olitsky had used the "wrong" virus for their experiment.

Harry Weaver went to Jonas Salk with a basic question: How many types of polio are there? Scientists thought there were at least two types, perhaps more. No one knew for sure how many types and strains there might be. A vaccine against one type of polio would not be a success if there were many different types.

Weaver wondered if Salk would be interested in investigating this problem. Certainly Salk was interested in taking part in the NFIP "typing program." Many virologists would have looked on this as a long, uncreative job. Salk saw it as his chance to gain some fame for the University of Pittsburgh. Of course, it also gave him the chance to run the laboratory of his dreams.

The National Foundation would give Salk a grant to pay for the typing program in Pittsburgh. Salk was told he would be able to plan and carry out the typing work himself. He would be given more room in the Municipal Hospital—and more laboratory workers. While the typing program was in its early stages, Salk started to learn as much as he could about poliovirus.

Salk's new laboratory would help with the typing of poliovirus. So would three other laboratories at the University of Kansas, the University of Utah, and the University of Southern California. Their work would be a major step in the development of a successful polio vaccine, but it would be far from exciting. In fact, before they started, two teams of scientists working elsewhere had already discovered the truth. There were only three types of polio. The Salk team and the other three laboratories were left with the task of dividing more than 100 *strains* of virus into these three types.

Salk was allowed more space in the basement and on

two other floors of the Municipal Hospital. Turning this area into a modern laboratory was going to be expensive. The Pittsburgh chapter of the March of Dimes wanted to give $35,000 raised in Pittsburgh. But this was against the rules. Only the national organization was supposed to grant money for research. So another foundation, the Sara Mellon Scaife Foundation, helped out with the costs of the laboratory.

Jonas and his wife, Donna, were now living in Wexford, a suburb of Pittsburgh. Their son Peter was four, and Darrell was one. Salk's wife once described Jonas as a perfectionist. He always had to have everything "just right." Unwilling to give the job to anyone else, Salk designed his new laboratory by himself.

It was clear to all who knew him that Salk would soon be experimenting with polio vaccines. Typing would never be enough for him. Of course, he wasn't dreaming of developing the Salk vaccine in 1949. But when he began work on the typing program, he just had to know more about this disease. He wanted to know what poliovirus did to the body and how the body answered back. Immunology was where his real interest lay.

Salk took some time selecting the staff members who would work in his new laboratory. Byron L. Bennett had already been working with him on the flu virus. They had met when Bennett was in the Army Medical Corps. He was always known by his nickname, "Major." Another key worker was Dr. Julius S. Youngner, a microbiologist from the University of Michigan. He was Salk's senior research associate. Dr. L. James Lewis, a bacteriologist, and Elsie Ward, a zoologist, were also part of the Salk team.

At that time, Salk's people greatly enjoyed working with him. Everyone understood that he or she was there to work, and Salk's appreciation made the job special.

When the typing began, Salk was thirty-four. He was made research professor of bacteriology at the medical school. At last, he had his own project and would be able to do things his way.

6

Typing the Virus

Jonas Salk had finally reached the point where he could run his own experiments in his own way. He was the "boss" in a fine, modern laboratory. The work was backed by grant money from the National Foundation for Infantile Paralysis. He had a staff of able, loyal assistants. Still, much of his work had to do with things other than actual laboratory activities.

Monkeys were one problem. Later, Harry Weaver said more progress might have been made in the fight against polio if monkeys had not been so hard to get. The monkeys used for polio experiments came from India and the Philippines. Sometimes they were sick or injured when they arrived. So Basil O'Connor directed his people to set up the Okatie Farm at Hardeeville, South Carolina. Laboratory monkeys were brought there. Okatie Farm made sure they were strong and well enough for laboratory use. Food for the

Thousands of Rhesus monkeys were used to help develop the polio vaccine.

laboratory animals was prepared and distributed by Okatie Farm, also.

More than 17,000 monkeys were used in the virus-typing work in which Salk's laboratory took part. Salk spent a lot of valuable time ironing out the system by which the animals were delivered to his laboratory. As head of the laboratory, he had to keep close track of the money he was spending on monkeys and other materials.

From the beginning, Salk was unhappy with the methods of typing poliovirus that everyone expected him to follow. Here is how it worked. Monkeys were infected with a strain that belonged to type 1. The animals that got well were inoculated with another virus, type unknown. If the monkeys became sick again, the unknown virus would have to belong to type 2 or type 3. Then the test would begin again. The unknown virus would be tried out on monkeys immune to type 2. If these monkeys became sick, the unknown virus probably belonged to type 3.

The tests were more difficult than they sound. How *much* virus should be given to a test monkey? The different strains of poliovirus were different from each other. Some were weak. And some were so powerful that the results of a particular test might not be clear.

Salk began thinking of other methods that could speed up the program. Researchers knew that a large amount of an unknown virus would cause a healthy animal to produce antibodies. They could then test these antibodies in samples of the animal's blood. They could check to see which type the unknown virus belonged to—type 1, type 2, or type 3. Salk believed this way of typing an unknown virus would save time and money. Fewer monkeys would be needed if tests were made by examining samples of blood.

When Salk tried to convince his fellow scientists that his

method was easier and faster, he ran into trouble. Dr. Albert Sabin was one who did not want to do things in a new way. Salk found that his new way of virus typing, developed through experiments on mice, only made the other researchers dislike him. They seemed to think of him as a newcomer, although he had worked with influenza viruses for years.

But Salk did not have to have everyone's approval in order to use both methods of typing the virus in his laboratory. He did the job he had been hired to do. But he also typed virus according to his own immunological method.

Dr. Albert Bruce Sabin continued to be Salk's strongest adversary. Sabin was a Jewish immigrant from eastern Europe who came to the United States when he was a boy. He graduated from the New York University medical school, just as Jonas Salk did, and he, too, became a researcher. Sabin was eight years older than Salk. He began working with poliovirus in the 1930s, when virology—the study of viruses—was still a fairly new science.

Always, Sabin firmly believed in a vaccine made from live but safe (because it had been weakened) poliovirus. He thought a killed-virus vaccine might make people immune for a short time. But he was afraid a dangerous live virus might suddenly appear in such a vaccine and cause paralysis or death.

For years, Sabin worked on the development of his own polio vaccine and spoke out against Salk's vaccine. He was sincerely opposed to the use of killed-virus vaccines. For his work in virology, he had earned the respect of other scientists long before Salk began to experiment with poliovirus.

One friend and important ally whom Salk met at this

Dr. Albert B. Sabin opposed the development of a killed-virus polio vaccine. He became world-famous for his development of a weakened but live-virus polio vaccine in 1960.

time was John Troan. Troan was a reporter who wrote about science for the *Pittsburgh Press* newspaper. Salk did not want Troan to write about his virus research and raise people's hopes too early. But when Troan published an article about the way polio researchers worked, Salk was pleased. He was glad to find someone who wrote the truth and did not make wild guesses about the future. Salk did not seem to trust most reporters or take pleasure in talking to them. He did not want them to know anything about his home life, either.

Harry Weaver was pleased with Jonas Salk. He asked Salk to speak in Washington, D.C., at a meeting of people who were working to raise money for the National Foundation. Salk turned out to be an excellent speaker. He was able to help nonscientists understand what polio research was all about. While talking to people after his speech, he showed his sense of humor and interest in the world outside of the laboratory. He knew science, of course, but he also was interested in music and the theater. He made other people feel he wanted to hear their opinions, too.

Salk knew he could speed up the virus-typing program. He started thinking of more exciting experiments. He was beginning to think seriously about ways of immunizing people against polio.

Another polio researcher, Isabel Morgan of Johns Hopkins University, had successfully carried out an important experiment. Morgan used poliovirus that had been treated with Formalin, a solution of the chemical formaldehyde. As a result of the treatment, the virus was no longer able to cause an infection. It was a "killed virus." Dr. Morgan found she could immunize monkeys with injections of her killed poliovirus.

Vaccines made of killed virus had been used before—with influenza, for example. But scientists like Sabin had long believed that poliovirus was different. They said it had to be "living," able to infect, in order to immunize anyone for any length of time. Many scientists were sure they knew the only way to prepare a poliovirus vaccine. The virus had to be treated in such a way that it could only cause a mild case. It should infect but not lead to paralysis.

Morgan realized that she had not solved the whole problem. Who could tell if her killed-virus vaccine would protect *humans* from polio? She also knew other scientists would want to see proof that there were no live viruses left in her vaccine.

In September 1949, Salk wrote a letter to Weaver. He asked if he could get some of Dr. Enders's virus that was growing in nonnervous tissue. Salk wanted to use it to immunize monkeys in an experiment. Weaver had to hold Salk back a little. He was afraid the men in charge of the virus-typing program would not want Salk to try a new experiment. Salk was supposed to be giving all his time and attention to the typing of poliovirus.

By the end of the 1940s, Salk was still working with influenza at Fort Dix, New Jersey. His program there was a study of how thousands of soldiers were getting along after receiving flu vaccines. A new IBM computer was now used to keep records of the soldiers' illnesses. Salk traveled often to New Jersey. Still, he felt that he had time to work on poliovirus. He wanted to grow the virus in nonnervous tissue, using Enders's method.

Dean McEllroy helped Salk get enough money to hire a specially trained laboratory worker. He also bought special supplies for his new experiments. When Harry Weaver came to Pittsburgh, he asked what Elsie Ward, a member of the Salk team, was working on. Salk told Weaver they were working with poliovirus, using Enders's method. Instead of becoming angry, Weaver got more National Foundation funds to help Salk do this work and the typing experiments, too.

In the spring of 1950, Salk wrote to Weaver to say that his new goal was to find a way of immunizing people against poliomyelitis. Salk believed it would not be long before someone would develop a vaccine and begin to test it on human beings. (At that time, scientists used people in mental institutions or prisons when they wanted to test new medicines.) The idea of testing a polio vaccine did not surprise Weaver. He knew that such tests would begin someday soon. Dr. Hilary Koprowski of the Lederle Laboratories company had already planned to give a live-virus vaccine to children in an institution.

What would happen after such test subjects had received a polio vaccine? Salk suggested that they should be given active virus. This would certainly show if they had become immune to polio or not. This was about the same thing Jenner had done long ago with matter from a smallpox blister.

In his letter to Weaver, Salk also discussed a strange idea. He thought it might be possible to immunize cows in order to develop milk that contained antibodies. He was thinking of all possible ways, even farfetched ones, by which polio could be stopped.

On July 12, 1950, Salk sent an application for a new grant to the National Foundation. He called attention to experiments at Johns Hopkins. Scientists there had shown that polio, like other infectious diseases, would cause the body to produce antibodies. Salk planned to test gamma globulin on monkeys to see if it would protect the animals from polio. (Gamma globulin is taken from the blood of many blood donors. It contains antibodies against many diseases.)

In his grant application, Salk said he planned to test eggs from immunized hens and milk from immunized cows. And, of course, he would be trying to develop a virus vaccine that could immunize without paralyzing anyone.

Salk received his National Foundation grant and began work in 1951. Because of Enders's breakthrough, scientists

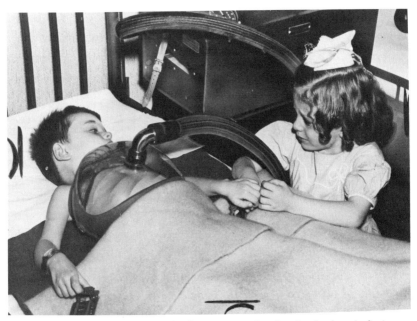

A five-year-old girl visits her younger brother in the hospital. A special chest respirator helps him breathe. Every summer in the 1940s and the early 1950s, fear swept through the country as parents worried that their children might catch polio.

like Salk would soon be able to make large amounts of poliovirus. Salk was still traveling back and forth to Fort Dix, working on his flu vaccine project. But he was also getting ready to produce poliovirus in a tissue culture. (A *culture* is the material in which bacteria or viruses are grown in laboratories.)

Meanwhile, a new scientist had come to the University of Pittsburgh. Dr. William McDowell Hammon had been appointed professor of epidemiology in the university's new Graduate School of Public Health. Hammon was a well-known virologist. He had worked with Enders on a vaccine to immunize cats against the distemper disease. Hammon had been working on polio antibody before he went to Pittsburgh. He was very interested in the idea of using gamma globulin to give humans some antibody against polio.

Hammon and Salk worked on the same disease—in the same building. Yet they never became friends.

In 1951, Hammon and other researchers successfully used gamma globulin to keep monkeys with polio from becoming paralyzed. The National Foundation set up a new program, and 55,000 children were given shots of gamma globulin. This substance might be helpful, and scientists knew it would not hurt anyone. In fact, the shots did give children immunity for a matter of weeks but not for longer.

Later, in 1952, Basil O'Connor made a bold move. With National Foundation funds, he bought up all the gamma globulin in the United States. Then he provided it free of charge to public health officers in places where polio epidemics were expected. It probably did prevent many children from being paralyzed that year.

Gamma globulin was expensive, and it did not give protection against polio for more than a few weeks. But its success showed that even small amounts of antibody would work against polio in humans. This was a very important finding. Hammon received and deserved a lot of credit for his work with gamma globulin.

In Salk's laboratory, Julius Youngner and Elsie Ward were working with the tissue cultures of poliovirus that Enders had first grown. It was exciting work. Salk and his people tried to grow many different strains of virus in their laboratory.

To prepare a vaccine, researchers had to use strains of virus belonging to each of the three types of poliovirus: type 1, type 2, and type 3. In his work, Salk used the Mahoney strain, a type 1 virus from a nonparalytic patient in Ohio. His type 2 virus was the MEF-1 strain found in 1942 by scientists working with the American Middle East forces in Egypt. The Saukett strain was his type 3 virus. It came from a boy in the Municipal Hospital of Pittsburgh. (Saukett was a misspelling of the boy's last name: Sarkett.)

Sometimes, National Foundation grantees and scientist-advisers gathered together to talk over the work they were doing. In March 1951, at a meeting in Hershey, Pennsylvania, the scientists talked about using human beings in experiments with vaccines. At this meeting, Dr. Hilary Koprowski of Lederle Laboratories reported that he had already tested a vaccine on twenty children and two adults. His subjects had not become sick, and they had produced antibodies.

Koprowski was using attenuated, or weakened, live poliovirus in his vaccine. Howard A. Howe, at Johns Hopkins University, had vaccinated chimpanzees and found antibodies in their blood. Now Koprowski had shown the same result with human subjects.

Still, some of the most important researchers working

on poliovirus did not want to go beyond learning everything they could about polio, including ways people became immune to the disease. They had no desire to try to develop a vaccine that would be mass-produced.

Jonas Salk was chosen to make a speech at the Second International Poliomyelitis Congress describing his work on the virus-typing program. This important meeting took place in Denmark, in September 1951. It was an honor for Salk to have been chosen to speak by the Typing Committee of the National Foundation.

He sailed to Europe on a ship called the *Stockholm*. John Enders, Albert Sabin, and other researchers were going to the congress, also. On the ship, Sabin was friendly to Salk. He said he would like to have a polio research institute. He even suggested that Salk could work with him. Salk was completely uninterested. He wanted the other researchers to think well of him. However, he would not have dreamed of going to work for anyone else.

At the meeting in Denmark, Enders spoke about his tissue-culture experiments. In his remarks, he included praise for Salk, who had used virus grown in test tubes to make experimental vaccines.

After Enders's speech, Salk stood up to say how much he owed to Enders. He told how he had been able to use nonnervous tissue from a monkey to prepare 200 tubes in which the poliovirus would grow. The old way of growing poliovirus would have used up 200 monkeys!

In his speech, Sabin warned his fellow scientists against expecting too much too soon. He said he was afraid things might take place in the human body that did not happen in tissue culture. It seemed as if Sabin would never think any of Salk's work was solid, useful research.

Salk spoke about the virus-typing program, as he had

been asked to do. He told the scientists it was not likely that more than three types of poliovirus would ever be found.

The trip back to the United States on the *Queen Mary* was a memorable one for Salk. Although he had met Basil O'Connor before, they had never really had an opportunity to get to know each other. Salk and O'Connor discovered they had many of the same interests and ideas. This was the beginning of a close friendship that was important to both men. The result of their friendship would also be important to many people who would never know them.

Later, Salk told Richard Carter (the author of *Breakthrough*) just how much he valued O'Connor:

> It is precisely O'Connor's assistance that makes it possible for me to do more than could possibly be done without his assistance. From the standpoints of science and society, then, O'Connor is an invaluable facility [very valuable person who can get things done], a rare item of human equipment. Name another like him. There is none. In him are combined self-interest and social interest in ideal proportions. He can't satisfy the first without fulfilling the other. And I come along and we hit it off and we discover that the relationship enables us to be more creative than we could have been without it.

O'Connor summed up his feelings about Salk:

> Jonas is in touch with the world. I don't mean that he's worldly. He's not.... But he is a human scientist, or call him humane or humanitarian or humanistic. He is aware of the world and concerned about it. He sees beyond the microscope....

7

Planning the Tests

When Salk returned from Europe, he began experiments using polioviruses on monkeys. He used the three strains of virus he had selected. He searched for the best monkey tissue to use in growing poliovirus. Then he had to learn just how much Formalin to use to kill the virus. How long would it take? What should the temperature be? Finally, there had to be a good way to test each "batch" of virus. Salk wanted to be sure not a single live virus remained in the vaccine.

Patiently, the Salk team studied the chemical reaction that took place between the virus and the Formalin. Salk tried out hundreds of different amounts of tissue-cultured virus and Formalin. He tried other possible methods of killing the virus, so it would immunize but not make anyone sick. Using monkey kidneys, he learned to grow the large amounts of virus that were needed for his important tests.

In December 1951, the Immunization Committee of the

National Foundation for Infantile Paralysis met in New York City. Among the members of the committee were Jonas Salk, David Bodian, John Enders, Thomas Francis, William Hammon, and Albert Sabin. Basil O'Connor, Thomas Rivers, and Harry Weaver were at the meeting, too. During the discussion, Salk and others said that the experiments on humans should be carried out with an inactive virus that could not infect. Again, Sabin spoke against the idea of using a killed-virus vaccine. It was his belief that the best vaccine would be one made from a live, but weakened, virus.

Howard Howe of Johns Hopkins University reported that he had tested a Formalin-treated vaccine on six children. His vaccine was made from viruses grown in the spinal cords of monkeys. Howe was interested in adding a mineral-oil adjuvant. That would make his vaccine produce more antibodies. But his experiments worried the other scientists. No one else believed in the use of nervous tissue that might cause allergic brain reactions.

Salk and his team worked in the laboratory day and night. They knew that soon they would try to vaccinate human beings against polio, using their experimental vaccines.

Salk had developed several possible kinds of vaccines. They were made in different ways. He tried different monkey tissues. He tried using one type of poliovirus, then all three types. In some of his vaccines, the viruses were treated with chemicals for different numbers of days.

Later, many reporters retold Donna Salk's story of how busy Jonas was. One night, she was trying to talk to him. When she said, "You're not even listening to me," Jonas smiled and answered, "My dear, you have my undevoted attention."

In the past, scientists working on poliomyelitis had

believed the virus spread to the spinal cord and brain through nerve fibers (part of the nervous system). They had not known that the virus really traveled from the intestines of sick persons to their central nervous systems. Until this was understood, a vaccine had seemed out of the question.

Now, in 1952, the National Foundation's Immunization Committee met again. Scientists at this meeting discussed how polio vaccines might work. If antibodies were present in the blood, they would attack the polioviruses in the blood. This, in turn, would prevent the infection from spreading from the intestines to the central nervous system. If that happened, paralysis could not take place.

At this meeting, Salk reported on the work he was doing, using Formalin to kill the poliovirus.

Salk's experiments on children began in June 1952. He found his first subjects at the D. T. Watson Home for Crippled Children at Leetsdale, near Pittsburgh. The home was a good place for handicapped boys and girls. Many of them had been crippled by polio. The people who worked there were interested in Salk's experiments. So were the children's parents. Salk began by giving vaccines to children who had had polio of the *same type* as the virus in the vaccine. They were already immune to that type of virus. Salk wanted to find out if the vaccine would increase the number of antibodies already in their blood.

These experiments were not written up in the newspapers. On June 12, Salk took blood from forty-five children and twenty-seven staff members of the Watson Home. He found out what types of antibodies were in the blood samples. Then he went back to the home on July 2 and gave polio vaccine to the children. That night, Salk went back to the home again, to see if the children were all right. There had been no problems. "When you inoculate children with a polio vaccine," he said later, "you don't sleep well for two or three months."

In his next experiment, Salk used all three types of virus to vaccinate children who had no polio antibody in their blood. This was more risky. This was a true experiment. Would humans produce antibodies the way chimpanzees had? Had the first children been safe only because they already had antibodies in their blood?

The answer pleased Salk and his team. The children who already had antibodies in their blood produced more. Children who had had no antibodies before they were vaccinated now had antibodies in their blood! In fact, they had enough antibodies to protect them from living polioviruses. Salk always called this "the thrill of my life." Now he knew for sure that a vaccine would stop the disease that had once seemed too mysterious for scientists to understand.

The children at the Watson Home liked Salk. He made friends with everyone there. When the experiment was over, he thanked them all for their help. He was especially thankful for their help in keeping his experiments with polio vaccine a secret. Only O'Connor, Weaver, and Rivers of the National Foundation knew what Salk was doing with his vaccines from July through December 1952.

The busy time had not yet come to an end. Salk carried out more secret experiments at the Polk State School, a home for mentally retarded people. He tried out a vaccine including all three types of virus. Most of the Polk School subjects were in their teens and twenties. The vaccine worked just fine.

At the same time, Salk and his staff were getting ready to make larger amounts of vaccine. A new worker, Percival "Val" Bazeley, came from Australia to join the team. Val figured out ways to use larger flasks (containers) and improve the whole tissue-culture process.

The children at the Watson School were tested again. In December, they still had the same numbers of antibodies they had had in September.

The next year, 1953, began with another meeting in Hershey, Pennsylvania. Salk announced that he had vaccinated human beings with killed-virus vaccines. Of course, the other scientists questioned him about the experiments. They wanted to know all about his use of adjuvants. They asked about the monkey-kidney tissue in which the virus had been grown. Should another, larger test be the next step? Sabin said he hoped more work would be done with laboratory animals first.

Enders was one of the scientists who felt that Salk should do more smaller tests. He was against the idea of a "field trial" of many people. He felt more work should be done to make sure the vaccines were safe.

In fact, Salk was not ready to ask for large field trials in January 1953. He did not have enough vaccine ready to try out on thousands of people. What he did have was confidence. He believed in himself and his work.

The 1953 March of Dimes drive to raise money was in progress. Weaver told the Board of Trustees of the National Foundation that a polio vaccine was coming soon. At the same time, both Weaver and Salk wanted to hold down the publicity. Weaver worried about the next polio season. Time was passing. How many people would come down with polio and become paralyzed while scientists talked to each other? He wanted to push ahead.

The National Foundation could not approve the field tests of a vaccine unless scientists and physicians also approved of them. What if something went wrong? Then the National Foundation would have trouble raising more money. Rivers believed Salk's best vaccine should be tested soon. But leading scientists had to approve the field trials before the foundation could go ahead with them.

A special meeting was held in New York City on February 26, 1953. The highest officials of the foundation were there. So were many other important people—scientists, physicians, teachers, and business people.

O'Connor and Rivers spoke. They told everyone about Salk's first experiments on humans. Salk also made a speech. With charts and graphs, he explained his experiments at the Watson Home and the Polk State School. He explained how he had prepared the inactivated virus. He also told the audience that a mineral-oil adjuvant had caused the children's bodies to produce a larger amount of antibody.

Salk's first article about his experiments was going to be printed in the *Journal of the American Medical Association* (*JAMA*) in March. Soon every American would learn about his experiments. They could not be kept secret much longer. Everyone would want the vaccine. People wanted anything that would protect their children from polio.

Rivers wanted to test Salk's vaccine again, as soon as possible. He knew Salk did not have enough vaccine ready for large numbers of people. But he wanted the audience at this meeting to start thinking about field trials. Salk suggested that the next step might be to vaccinate around 25,000 children to see if the vaccine was safe for widespread use. He added that he was not ready to say right then and there that 25,000 children was the right number for a test. He just wanted to vaccinate as many children as possible *before the polio season.* If shots were given during the polio season and some children came down with polio, the vaccine might be blamed. Then people would be so afraid of the new vaccine that it would never get a fair test.

After the meeting, it was agreed that Rivers would write a letter to *JAMA*. He would explain that there could not be any nationwide use of a polio vaccine for many months. Perhaps this would keep people from getting too excited about the vaccine when they read about it in the newspapers.

Then something strange happened. A writer named Earl Wilson put a story about polio in his newspaper column. He called it "New Polio Vaccine—Big Hopes Seen." This happened *before* Salk's article came out in *JAMA*. Salk was so upset that he hurried to New York City to talk to Basil O'Connor about the publicity. Salk thought it might be helpful for him to go on the radio and talk about polio research in general. A nationwide radio network broadcast was set for the night of March 26. The title of Salk's speech was "The Scientist Speaks for Himself."

Basil O'Connor opened the radio show. He talked about the National Foundation for Infantile Paralysis and its different programs. Of course, he described the medical research program of which Salk was a part. Then he introduced Dr. Jonas E. Salk.

This was the first time most Americans had heard of Salk. They were not used to listening to scientists talk on the radio. O'Connor said Salk would tell about all the researchers who were working in their laboratories to win the fight against polio.

Speaking clearly, using simple terms nonscientists could understand, Salk made his first report to the public. He announced that studies were going on using a polio vaccine on human subjects. Then he went over the history of polio research. He told how polio was first given to an experimental animal, how it was found to be caused by more than one virus, and how, in 1951, scientists knew they had just three types of poliovirus to deal with. Salk explained that a person had to be immune to all three types for complete prevention of polio. He told about the discovery that poliovirus enters through the mouth or nose and then reaches the nervous system through the blood. He explained how antibodies from the blood of a sick animal could be used to stop polioviruses from attacking the nervous system of another animal. He also told how gamma globulin from human blood had been used to protect some children during the past summer.

Polio was not very different from other diseases caused by viruses, Salk said. He went over the basic facts about vaccination:

> Now, the principle of vaccination is not difficult to understand. A vaccine is made of the virus that causes the disease. Then, when the vaccine is injected, the body reacts with the formation of antibodies. These antibodies are found in the blood and remain to defend against future attacks....[T]he virus contained in the vaccine must be rendered [made] harmless so that when injected it will not cause disease but will result only in the formation of protective antibodies. [Of course, this was one of the major points on which Salk and Sabin disagreed.]

In addition, Salk went over Enders's discovery that all three types of poliovirus could be grown in a culture of living tissue. And he explained how he had used a mineral-oil adjuvant, mixed with a virus, in developing flu vaccines for the army.

At the close of his speech, Salk said that no vaccine would be available for widespread use during the next polio season. "Certain things cannot be hastened, since each new step cannot be made without establishing first the wisdom of the one before. We are now faced with facts and not merely with theories. With this new enlightenment we can now move forward more rapidly and with more confidence."

The next day's newspapers helped Salk spread the word that polio would not be ended during the summer of 1953. In his *JAMA* article (April 4), Salk explained that it took a lot of time to prepare and study each new batch of experimental vaccine. Only then could shots be given to the public. Safety was his aim. And the work could not be hurried.

Salk worried that something might go wrong, and it did. A drug-producing company, Parke, Davis & Co., made a surprising announcement. The company said it would soon begin to produce the "new vaccine" that Dr. Jonas Salk had "discovered." Salk, who had done some work for Parke, Davis during the development of the mineral-oil adjuvant for the flu vaccine, was worried about this newspaper story. It was very unfair to him. People would think he was developing a polio vaccine just to make money for a company.

The April 4 issue of *JAMA* included another Salk story, this time about the flu vaccine, which had been effective. It had been successfully used for more than two years now. *JAMA* also published a letter from Rivers. Rivers wanted to make sure no one would expect a polio vaccine ready for public use for some time yet.

Salk was famous as soon as he had made his radio speech, but he did not encourage publicity. The news stories soon slowed down, and he was able to go back to work in the laboratory.

In the spring of 1953, Salk followed an old custom of immunologists. He vaccinated his wife Donna, himself, and his three sons. He gave the boys injections while they slept in order not to frighten them. Peter was nine, Darrell was six, and Jonathan—the youngest person ever to receive a polio vaccination—was three. Then Salk began some new experiments at the Watson Home. He was now planning on nationwide field trials of a polio vaccine.

Weaver was also making detailed plans for field trials. He thought they should take place before May 1954. He had even planned a new committee to help run field tests and study the results for the National Foundation. When Salk learned about Weaver's plans, he was annoyed. He asked to be included in any future discussions. Salk, O'Connor, and Weaver met to "make up." They agreed that field trials in 1954 were necessary if a vaccine was to be ready for public use in time for the 1955 polio season.

Basil O'Connor had been fighting polio for more than twenty years. It is no wonder that he was pushing for the tests. It seemed all that was needed was a vaccine that could be produced in large amounts. But Salk had to explain that he and his co-workers were still testing many elements of the polio vaccine. They just were not yet sure how long to treat the virus with Formalin. Another problem was the mineral oil to be mixed with the killed virus. All these matters called for time, testing, and patience. He had to be sure it worked safely.

As usual, O'Connor did not demand that the work be speeded up. But he asked Salk if it might be possible to have field trials by the end of 1953 or the beginning of 1954. Salk said it was possible.

A new Vaccine Advisory Committee began its work in the spring of 1953. The members talked about holding field trials all over the United States. The NFIP's Immunization Committee had included scientists such as Albert Sabin and William Hammon who did not believe a vaccine made from inactivated virus would be useful at all. But the Vaccine Advisory Committee had been created to make progress.

O'Connor and Rivers were tired of waiting for scientists to agree on the "perfect" vaccine.

Dr. Joseph A. Bell of the National Institutes of Health was chosen to help the NFIP plan its field tests. Weaver had been sure that schoolchildren who volunteered to be vaccinated would be the subjects of the field trials. Perhaps, only upper-class and middle-class families would agree to have their children take part. Having fewer children from poor neighborhoods might somehow change the results of the trials. Bell had to plan carefully.

Were the tests to be truly scientific? Then no one should know who had received the real vaccine and who had not. This was an important problem. If the people who gave the shots knew which children were receiving the real vaccine, there would surely be some "cheating." The physicians might, for example, try to see to it that their own friends and patients were vaccinated. Remember, anything that would possibly prevent polio seemed to be a miracle to most people. Every summer, fear of polio had swept across the nation. No one was cool about this subject. Feelings ran high among physicians and teachers, as well as parents.

There was another problem. What if the children who had received the real vaccine knew it? The minute any of those children took sick for any reason, people would say it was polio. They would blame the experimental vaccine. Scientists had to solve this problem before the field trials could begin.

The National Foundation people began to call for *double-blind* tests. In a double-blind test, every volunteer would be given an injection. Half of the shots would be vaccine. The other half of the shots would be a placebo—a completely harmless substance that did nothing whatever to the body. This was the same method that had been used to test Francis's flu vaccine during World War II. *Who* received *what* would be kept secret. No one working on the field trials would know until the final results were announced. This way, people could not find fault with the vaccine along the way. The number of children who came down with polio after getting the vaccine shot would be measured against the number of children who came down with polio after getting the placebo shot. Only in this way could results of the tests be scientific proof and not just accidents.

On the other hand, Salk himself had doubts. He feared that the tests called for too much record keeping and secrecy. Would the tests become more important than the idea of saving children from death and paralysis? If it took too long to set up the tests, the polio season would begin again. Then no tests would be possible. Salk also wanted to take blood samples from the vaccinated children. He really wanted to go on improving the experimental vaccines during the tests. To do that, he would have to know if the vaccine produced antibodies in the children's blood. Finally, Salk simply did not like the idea of a placebo. He hated to think that so many children—half of the volunteers—would get a shot that could not protect them from polio.

Many scientists, led by Sabin, were against the killed-virus vaccine. Sabin was working on a weakened, live-poliovirus vaccine. Salk did not want his killed-virus experimental vaccines to fail right before the eyes of the whole world. If that should happen, killed-virus vaccines might never be given a chance again.

All during the preparations for the field trials, Sabin spoke out against Salk and the killed-virus vaccine. Sabin did not want any field trials before his own vaccine was ready. He said not enough was known about poliovirus yet. He said the type 1 Mahoney virus Salk used was very dangerous. He questioned how long killed-virus vaccines would prevent polio. He said his vaccine made with a "living" virus would make people immune for many years, if not for life.

The NFIP supported Sabin's research. O'Connor did not want to seem to favor any particular researcher over another. In fact, no one really wanted to attack Sabin or try to quiet him. After all, he had a right to say what he thought. Because of Sabin, the people planning the field trials had to be extra careful. There must be no flaws in the tests. If Salk's vaccine would not protect children, as Sabin said, then the trials must show it, before more time and money were spent.

Hart Van Riper, the medical director of the National Foundation, quarreled with Harry Weaver, the director of research, in the summer of 1953. Weaver left the National Foundation at a difficult time, just before the field trials.

In September, the Vaccine Advisory Committee met again in New York. Salk spoke to them about his latest tests of vaccine with and without adjuvant. The committee voted to test a vaccine without the mineral oil. It decided the virus should be given in two or three shots instead of one.

The Salk team was still trying out different combinations of virus, Formalin, temperature, and time. But someday soon they would have to choose the best vaccine for use in the field trials. Salk was working long hours, taking naps when he was too tired to go on, and eating sandwiches at his desk. He took an active part in all of the laboratory work. He was not a boss who gave an order and walked away. Fortunately, his chief assistant, Julius Youngner, developed a new test that could be used to tell if a virus was killing the tissue in a living tissue culture. This important test was really a short cut. Youngner helped everyone to speed up the work on experimental vaccines.

Now problems with the manufacture of vaccine needed

to be solved. If thousands of shots were to be given, a lot of vaccine had to be made. Salk and his people could never produce enough. Commercial (profit-making) laboratories would have to become involved. They could turn out huge batches of killed-virus vaccine, following Salk's directions. Salk was watchful, afraid the scientists who worked for the drug companies might think they knew a better way of making the vaccine. Salk wanted to be sure that more than one company helped to prepare the vaccine—and that all of them followed his methods. O'Connor agreed to talk to several big companies.

Always, Salk worried that plans for the polio vaccine and the field trials were being made more or less behind his back. He wrote letters to people such as O'Connor. He called the leaders of the National Foundation until they hated to answer the telephone. Basically, Salk wanted a simpler plan for the field trials. He suggested that pediatricians (physicians dealing with the care, development, and diseases of children) and even parents might be included in discussions of how to conduct the trials. He kept trying to talk the planners out of using placebos with some of the children. He was not trying to make trouble. But he sincerely wanted as many children as possible to be vaccinated. Children who got a placebo in their shot would not be protected against the poliovirus. If they later became infected with the virus, they might get polio and be paralyzed. O'Connor understood. After all, Salk was the father of three boys.

At the end of October, the epidemiologist Joseph Bell went back to his job at the U.S. Public Health Service. He was in favor of double-blind field trials, but no final decision had yet been made.

Next, O'Connor turned to an old associate, a public health physician named G. Foard McGinnes. McGinnes's new job at the National Foundation was to get together enough vaccine. He had to deal with scientists at the Parke, Davis company who were thinking of using another method of treating poliovirus instead of doing it Salk's way. Did they have in mind the production of a vaccine that Parke, Davis could sell as its own?

In the end, O'Connor met with several manufacturers, inviting them all to take part. Naturally, they had questions about *patents* and *royalties*. To take out a patent means to register an idea and design with the government. A patent is a government document giving the inventor rights to the invention for a limited time. A patent gives the inventor the right to prevent others from making, using, or selling the invention. Royalties are payments made to an inventor for each item sold under a patent. O'Connor told the manufacturers that the NFIP would not let its grantees—the scientists it gave grants to—take out patents or earn royalties from their discoveries. Salk's vaccine could be made by anyone who was able to produce it, if it passed the field tests.

There was no easy-to-follow recipe for Salk's polio vaccine. Other scientists tried to make a vaccine Salk's way and failed. In November 1953, for example, one group of scientists led by Dr. Albert Milzer reported that they had tried but could not inactivate the poliovirus with Formalin. They believed an ultraviolet method of making the virus inactive was safer than Salk's.

In November, O'Connor announced to the press that field trials of a polio vaccine would begin in February 1954. Second-grade children (who had the most polio of all ages) would be vaccinated before the polio season began. The results would be based on a comparison. The number of vaccinated second-graders who came down with polio would be set against the number of unvaccinated children in grades one and three who had the disease. This was Salk's favorite plan.

Right away, people began to disagree with O'Connor. He had expected his organization to judge the results of the field trials. But some people did not want the National Foundation to "grade" its own test. Was there a scientist who did not work for the foundation who could handle this job? A man was chosen to study the field trials and then give a completely fair report of what had taken place. He was Salk's former teacher, Dr. Thomas Francis.

Hart Van Riper asked Francis if he would do it. The National Foundation was ready to give the University of Michigan a grant to cover the costs. Van Riper and O'Connor met with Francis and talked to him about the field trials. Right away, Francis brought up the idea of a double-blind trial. He believed that it would be the fairest and most reliable kind of a test. Without the use of a placebo on half the children, the results of the trials might be uncertain.

After Francis and Salk discussed the best way to test the vaccine, Salk changed his mind. He agreed that a double-blind field test would be the best. Anyone connected with the National Foundation had much to lose if the tests failed. But Francis had nothing to lose, either way. Salk had complete faith that Francis would not let any personal feelings get in the way of doing a good job. Francis would plan and carry out a perfect experiment, no matter how large the project became.

After weeks of thinking it over, Francis decided to take on the work O'Connor had asked him to do. Only one thing could not go the way he wanted. In some states, O'Connor had already planned to carry out the vaccinations without a control group. This meant that there would not be a group of children there who received a placebo. In these states, another plan would have to be followed. State health officers had already agreed to it.

Francis set up his evaluation center in January 1954 at the University of Michigan. One thing was clear. No results would be revealed to anyone until Francis was ready to make his report on the field trials. The vaccinations were to be given before the 1954 polio season. The results would not be announced before the spring of 1955, a year after the vaccinations were given.

The companies lined up to make the vaccine for the field trials were Parke, Davis; Eli Lilly; Cutter Laboratories; Wyeth Laboratories; and Pitman-Moore. Salk found it impossible to give them a simple recipe for preparing the vaccine. It was not easy to move his vaccine-making methods from a small laboratory to a large company.

William Workman of the U.S. Public Health Service was keeping an eye on the trials. The government would license the vaccine if it worked. It could then be manufactured and sold everywhere. The government's National Institutes of Health (NIH) had to be in on the project from the beginning. When some drug companies had trouble making the same vaccine Salk had made, the government's health people began to worry about safety. People at the NIH wanted a germ killer known as Merthiolate added to the vaccine. Salk objected. He had not been using Merthiolate and did not know what it would do to the vaccine. But the NIH would not allow the vaccine to be given unless it had some Merthiolate in it.

8

Volunteers and Polio Pioneers

Suddenly, a new phrase began to appear in newspaper and magazine articles about poliomyelitis. Reporters were writing about "the Salk vaccine." This did not please Jonas Salk at all! He knew other scientists well—especially those who had worked with poliovirus. They would feel that he was taking credit for work done by many people. He begged O'Connor to tell the publicity people at the National Foundation for Infantile Paralysis not to give his name to the polio vaccine. But Salk was fast becoming a public figure, and there was nothing he or anyone else could do about it. His name and his picture would soon be known to millions of people in the United States—and in many other lands as well.

Time was flying, and O'Connor had to change the dates of the field trials. They would take place in March or April, he said. For one thing, the companies producing the vaccine were still having trouble. Salk asked that every batch be

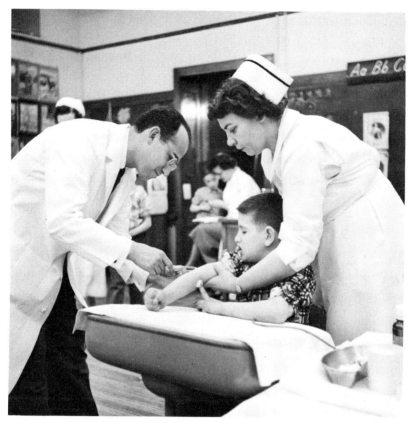

Dr. Jonas E. Salk gives a schoolchild in Pittsburgh, Pennsylvania, a shot of the killed-virus vaccine.

tested for safety. The National Foundation finally decided to use only Parke, Davis and Eli Lilly vaccine in the field trials.

On February 23, 1954, Salk began vaccinating schoolchildren in Pittsburgh, Pennsylvania. Five thousand children there were taking part in a test of the vaccine. Salk used vaccine made in his laboratory, but it was the same one now being manufactured by the drug companies. Dr. Salk himself injected 137 children, about one a minute. There were no problems with the vaccine.

But the difficulty of making an absolutely safe vaccine for the tests was far from over. Parke, Davis feared that some of its vaccine was spoiled. Time was lost again while the vaccine was retested for safety. It was found to be all right.

If the field trials did not start in April, it would be too late to test the vaccine in 1954. The polio season would begin in May.

Still, the National Institutes of Health (NIH) was not satisfied that all the vaccine had been fully tested for safety. The method used at one company had not been exactly right. On March 11, Sabin spoke before a meeting of physicians in the Michigan Medical Society. Again he told his story. He said inactivated polio vaccines might not work. But he, Sabin, was preparing a vaccine that would definitely work. It would infect people, yet not cause serious illness or paralysis. It would also result in immunity for life, just as if the subjects had lived through a case of polio. Of course, Sabin was worried about the upcoming field trials of the Salk vaccine.

The National Foundation had known that Sabin was going to speak on March 11. So people there arranged for Salk to give a speech on the same day. He appeared in New Orleans, before the New Orleans Graduate Medical Assembly. Salk told how he had by now successfully vaccinated seven thousand children. No child had suffered any harm. He added that booster shots were necessary for long-lasting immunization. He had given some children a second shot seven months after the first. But, because summer was coming, the field trials would be a little different. He planned to give all the shots in a shorter time. Salk told the physicians in Louisiana that a well-planned experiment never fails. He meant that, whatever happens, a good experiment reveals the truth.

On March 25, O'Connor and Rivers met with the director of the National Institutes of Health (NIH), Dr. W. H. Sebrell, Jr. Instead of telling O'Connor to begin the field trials, the NIH researchers wanted more thorough safety tests developed for use on all new vaccine. Each drug company would have to check its vaccine very carefully indeed. Salk himself was sure the vaccine for the field trials would be as safe as the vaccine he had made.

On Sunday, April 4, a well-known writer named Walter Winchell announced on radio and TV that the Salk vaccine was unsafe. Winchell said the U.S. Public Health Service had tested the Salk vaccine and found in it live poliovirus that killed several monkeys. He said, too, that the NFIP was trying to kill his story. There was nothing O'Connor could do. The foundation informed the public that no vaccine with live virus in it would be used in the trials. The U.S. Public Health Service also said that no unsafe vaccine would be used. Salk made a statement saying the vaccine was completely safe.

Amazingly, Winchell's "news" caused very little trouble for Salk and O'Connor. Only Minnesota withdrew from the trials, along with a few counties elsewhere.

One week before the vaccinations were supposed to begin, a new problem came up. The factory making needles for the shots of vaccine was closed down by a strike. But just in time it started production again.

The final decision to go ahead with the field trials was made by the U.S. Public Health Service on Sunday, April 25, 1954. Salk, O'Connor, and the members of the Vaccine Advisory Committee all met in Bethesda, Maryland, for one last discussion. The committee voted to let the field trials begin. A big step had been taken, and everyone hoped for the best. The great experiment began the next morning. Six-year-old Randy Kerr of Fairfax County, Virginia, was first in line to receive his shot—and a button that said "Polio Pioneer."

What were the field trials like? O'Connor gave Melvin A. Glasser, a sociologist, the job of administrative director of the tests. The task was to give a million children three shots of vaccine or placebo. Blood samples had to be taken from many of the children, also.

First, the children and their parents had to be told all about the trials. Why were scientists testing a vaccine? Why should people volunteer their children to be the "guinea pigs"—the subjects of scientific experiments? No child could take part without the permission of his or her parents. The volunteer helpers who would give the shots and keep the records had to be told what their responsibilities would be as well.

Nearly 20,000 physicians and public health officers, 40,000 registered nurses, 14,000 school principals, and 50,000 teachers volunteered to help. More than 200,000 other citizens pitched in—members of the National Foundation chapters across the country. Volunteers set up centers where children could be vaccinated. They drove people around, picked up the permission forms parents had to sign, worked with newspaper people, and helped the physicians and nurses in any way they could. They were not paid to do this. Other clubs and organizations also sent their members to help. Basil O'Connor was happy, but not surprised. The American people were working together, just as they had done during wartime.

Dorothy Ducas was the public relations director of the National Foundation, NFIP. She played an important part, creating printed materials that explained the field trials to ordinary people. For example, Ducas knew the word *experi-*

ment could not be in her materials. A test was one thing, but the idea of an experiment might frighten parents away.

In thirty-three states, second-graders were given polio vaccine. Other second-graders and children in grades one and three were not given any kind of a shot. These children were only studied so their health could be compared with that of the second-graders who were vaccinated. In eleven other states, real double-blind tests were run. Children in the first three grades of school had shots. But half got the trial vaccine and half received a placebo. Because of the two different kinds of tests, the foundation had to prepare two different sets of information for parents and children. The National Foundation passed out all kinds of things to the public. They created stories for newspapers, radio and TV scripts, and informative leaflets. They also prepared guides for schoolteachers and lists of important dates, places, and times.

Francis had planned the double-blind part of the field trials. The other part, where children who had no shots were studied and compared with vaccinated children, was also closely watched over by Francis and his assistants. Francis was not working, or even speaking, for the National Foundation. He had nothing to do with the companies that made the vaccine. He did not want any publicity, either. Comparing results, keeping records—these were the jobs of the scientists in Ann Arbor. No one knew the results of the field trials until they were announced. No one even talked about them.

There were three key questions the field trials would answer: How many vaccinated children got polio? How many of the children who received placebo came down with polio? How many of the children who had no shots at all got polio? Francis and his team looked into every case of polio

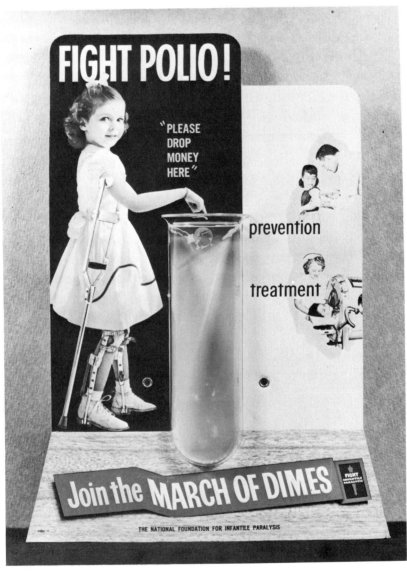

The March of Dimes Poster Child for 1954. Each year a child was selected to appear on posters asking people to contribute money to the fight against polio.

among the schoolchildren and their families and friends. When other people in a child's family got polio, they might have caught it from him or her. Scientists searched for poliovirus in blood samples from the children. Twenty-eight state laboratories in the United States worked on the field trials. Scientists wanted to see how many antibodies appeared in blood samples taken from children before the vaccinations, then seven weeks later, and again at the end of the polio season. All the information from the trials was put into IBM computers.

After the field trials began, Salk found that the Merthiolate in the vaccine was causing trouble. The vaccine was not working against type 1 virus. But it was too late to change the vaccine and start again. Once the trials had begun, a change would have ruined the results. Of course, he worried all the more about the test children because he knew about the problem with Merthiolate.

The National Foundation had to carry out a supercampaign to raise money that summer. Expenses had never been higher. The costs of making vaccine and keeping laboratories open were great. The cost of patient care was up, too, because of epidemics in the early 1950s. Also, O'Connor knew he would have to order the production of more vaccine for use *after* the field trials. He had to go ahead and promise to pay companies to make new vaccine. What was he going to do with it? O'Connor had so much faith in the vaccine, he planned to give it out free in 1955!

CHAPTER

9

An American Hero

Experts studying the number of polio cases in the country kept reporting that the number was down in 1954. But polio was tricky. This might simply mean that it was not going to be a bad polio year.

Right after the test children received their shots, the American Medical Association (AMA) began to complain. Private physicians were not happy to see a new vaccine provided free by the National Foundation for Infantile Paralysis. Many physicians were afraid the foundation would take away their patients. The field trials might make people think all medical care should be free. The physicians wanted to be paid for their work. But O'Connor had planned ahead so he could answer his critics. He had made sure some important physicians approved the vaccine testing. In fact, one member of the Vaccine Advisory Committee was on the Board of Trustees that directed the AMA. A lot of physicians had volunteered to take part in the field trials, too.

In September 1954, Salk went to the Third International Poliomyelitis Conference in Rome, Italy. O'Connor, Rivers, Francis, Sabin, Hammon, Enders, and others were there. At this meeting, the old quarrel between live-virus people and killed-virus people broke out again. Salk read a paper about his vaccines. Again, he explained the basis for his vaccine. He said a virus did not have to cause sickness in order to result in antibody production in the bloodstream. Then he explained what would happen when a person had had one or two shots of antigen (his killed virus). Whenever a new infection entered the body, it would respond to the "foreigners" with a flood of protective antibodies. Salk believed he knew the way to give people immunity that would last. This could be done if shots were given at several different times. (The shots a person would receive after the first shot were called *booster shots*.)

Albert Sabin spoke next. He reported on his kind of vaccine—one made of live viruses that had been weakened. Hilary Koprowski also said live-virus vaccines would win out over the others. The scientists talking about vaccines at the Third International Conference all seemed to "choose up sides" and back either Salk or Sabin.

Salk still had many problems to solve. Merthiolate made his vaccine useless against type 1 virus. But when the Vaccine Advisory Committee wanted to remove it from the vaccine, the National Institutes of Health (NIH) refused. The NIH said no proof had been shown that the vaccine would be safe without Merthiolate. Early in 1955, Salk and the vaccine-manufacturing companies tried to get proof. Thousands of children not involved in the field trials received shots just to make sure a vaccine not containing Merthiolate could be safely used. The vaccine worked well, as Salk had known it would.

Dr. Thomas Francis, Jr., and Dr. Jonas E. Salk, in early 1955.

Francis expected to finish his study of the field trials and make an announcement in April 1955. The plan was to call a meeting of important scientists, physicians, and public health officers. The Eli Lilly company said it would set up a closed-circuit (not public) television show so other physicians all over the United States could view Francis's announcement. Finally, it was decided that the meeting would take place in Ann Arbor, at the University of Michigan. The university's Public Relations Department made plans for all the radio and TV people who would surely be there to hear the big news.

Meanwhile, 9,000 children in Pittsburgh had had their

booster shots. In January 1955, Salk reported that none of them had become sick with polio.

Salk then appeared on Edward R. Murrow's "See It Now" television program to answer the public's questions about the field trials. He called the vaccine "a poliomyelitis vaccine." He did *not* call it "the Salk vaccine." He talked about all the scientists from different fields who had made the development of a vaccine possible: virologists, microbiologists, biochemists, and biophysicists. People who watched Salk on TV liked him and believed what he said. They were not going to call the vaccine anything but "the Salk vaccine." Salk was a good, clear speaker whom they could understand. He seemed to be a modest man. Everyone began to expect good news from Francis.

The imporant meeting and announcement were set for April 12. This date would be the tenth anniversary of Franklin Roosevelt's death. O'Connor's friend and partner had died of a stroke while visiting Warm Springs in April 1945. Roosevelt had been serving his fourth term as president when he died. Many Americans would be thinking of President Roosevelt on the day Francis reported on the first polio vaccine.

Donna Salk did not usually go with her husband to scientific gatherings. But Salk invited her and the boys to come to the meeting in Ann Arbor.

More than 500 scientists and physicians heard Francis read his report on the Salk vaccine. Their applause was controlled. But around the building, where reporters and students were waiting to hear the news, tremendous excitement swept the crowd.

Francis's 128-page report told of the results from using different testing methods and different targets—type 1 virus, type 2 virus, and type 3 virus. Salk knew at once that

News reporters crowd the room as the announcement about the safety and effectiveness of the polio vaccine is made. From left to right: Dr. Jonas E. Salk, Dr. Thomas Francis, Jr., and Basil O'Connor.

the vaccine had not been exactly the same in every batch made by the drug companies. Although Merthiolate was not mentioned, he knew the vaccine had worked best against the type 2 and type 3 viruses.

At the end of the report, Francis pointed out that he could not sum up the performance of the vaccine as a whole. Speaking of the parts of the country where the double-blind trial had taken place, he reported that the vaccine was 80 to 90 percent effective against paralytic poliomyelitis. It was 60 to 70 percent effective against type 1 virus and 90 percent *or more* effective against type 2 and type 3 viruses.

News reporters liked the first sentences of the report handed to them by the university. It simply said, "The vaccine works. It is safe, effective, and potent [powerful]." This was really all most people wanted to hear.

After Francis had read the report—it took well over an hour—Salk read a paper he had written. When he got up to speak, everyone in the audience stood up and clapped for him. He began by praising Francis for the excellence of his report. Then he went on to mention many of the scientists with whom he had worked. But he did not say a word about his own people in the Virus Research Laboratory at the University of Pittsburgh. His assistants, who were in Ann Arbor, were very hurt.

"Vaccination Against Paralytic Poliomyelitis: Performance and Prospects" was the title of Salk's paper. Of course, it had been written before he or anyone else knew what was in Francis's report. Salk went on and on about a new, better plan: two shots given two to four weeks apart and a third shot given seven months later. He also talked about the way Merthiolate had lessened the protection the vaccine gave against type 1 virus. Finally, he claimed that new vaccines and ways of giving the shots could be 100 percent effective against paralysis caused by polio.

This claim was shocking to the other scientists. Salk was talking about vaccines that had not been tested yet. Why had he felt it was necessary to give such a speech on such an important day? Both Francis and Rivers were very annoyed.

After Salk had finished, William Workman of the National Institutes of Health gathered a group of scientists together to discuss the federal licensing of Salk's vaccine. After a two-hour meeting, Workman announced that everyone wanted to license the vaccine. The secretary of health, education, and welfare, Oveta Culp Hobby, signed the official papers that very evening. Thanks to O'Connor, vaccine was ready and waiting to be used.

The moment Francis reported that the Salk vaccine worked, Jonas Salk became an American hero. After all, this day had been a long time coming. Many people had faithfully sent in their dimes and dollars to the March of Dimes for years. The vaccine had been developed through hard, step-by-step laboratory work by scientists who were just "doing their job." Still, it seemed like a miracle to people who had never expected to see it in their lifetimes.

It was months before the excitement died down and Salk could concentrate on his own thoughts again. On the day of the announcement, people throughout the United States celebrated in all kinds of ways. School principals called assemblies and announced the victory over polio to their children. Many people went to temples and churches to thank God for Dr. Salk. Horns honked. Bells rang. And plenty of tears were shed.

Reporters working for newspapers and radio and TV stations were glad Jonas and Donna Salk were a nice, friendly couple with three good-looking boys. In hundreds of stories, the reporters told about Salk's "discovery" of a vaccine that would end a twentieth-century plague and bring peace to the hearts of Americans. Especially, they told how hard Salk had worked to make sure the vaccine was safe before he let it be used on children.

People showered Salk and his family with letters and telegrams. He received all kinds of presents, too. The gifts included money, candy, and flowers. People felt he was their personal friend, and they sent him photographs of their families. He was offered jobs in the government and jobs with private companies. A hospital changed its name to Jonas E. Salk Memorial Hospital. A school was named after

Salk immediately became world-famous when the polio vaccine was pronounced safe and effective.

him. People named babies after him. Hollywood movie studios wanted to make movies of his life story.

The organizers of a parade in New York City asked Salk and his parents to take part. Salk said no and added that his father was not well. Nevertheless, the parade organizers picked his mother and father up the next morning. They not only rode in the parade, but had a good time doing it.

Among the honorary degrees Salk was offered were degrees from the University of Pittsburgh, the City College of New York, and New York University. Mount Sinai Hospital, where he had been an intern, gave him a special medal. The state of Pennsylvania and the Congress of the United States also gave him awards. Although Salk was nominated for a Nobel Prize in medicine, he did not win it. He did, however, receive a citation from President Dwight Eisenhower.

In *Newsweek* (April 25, 1955), Americans read about "A Quiet Young Man's Magnificent Victory." The article described Salk as "a dark-eyed, slightly built, and quietly intense man who wears glasses and has a highly developed sense of privacy." After Francis's announcement, said *Newsweek*, "Salk's name became as secure a word in the medical dictionary as those of such predecessors as Jenner, Pasteur, Schick, and Lister."

The *New York Times Magazine* (July 17, 1955) carried a long story about "the man who developed the polio vaccine and became almost a folk hero overnight." This story said that:

> Salk is profoundly disturbed by the torrent of fame that has descended upon him. He is trying hard to keep himself and the scientific method with which he identifies himself from being sucked into a whirlpool of

Jonas Salk with his sons, Peter (left), Jonathan, and Darrell, and his wife, Donna.

publicity, politics and pressures of various sorts. He talks continually about getting out of the limelight and back to his laboratory. "It's not a question of modesty," he says, "I want to clean up this vaccine job and get on to other things."

The article also told about Salk and his family at the White House:

One of the few invitations Dr. Salk had accepted was from the President. Later Salk told a friend, "There we stood, my wife, my three boys and myself, in the rose garden of the White House while the President congratulated me. I thought to myself, 'What am I doing here?' I'd been told beforehand to confine my reply to a straight thank you, but I couldn't do it. I felt I had to acknowledge my associates and all those others who had made the vaccine possible. So I said what I felt."

"My family took it all pretty much in stride, although that night the boys were kidding around when suddenly Peter [aged eleven] said, 'My goodness—I met the President today!' It was really very nice."

In the end, most of Salk's well-wishers were answered with a simple "Thanks, but I cannot accept the gift." Almost immediately, he decided he would rather be working in his laboratory than standing on a platform talking to a group of people. And he was very sensitive to the fact that his fellow scientists did not like all the attention he was getting.

Never at any time did Salk try to make money from his vaccine. Salk, Francis, and Alan Gregg of the Rockefeller Foundation appeared on another "See It Now" television program. Edward R. Murrow asked Francis and Salk who held the patent on his vaccine. Salk's answer became famous:

"Well, the people, I would say. There is no patent. Could you patent the sun?"

Over and over again, when he did accept a special honor, Salk told the audience that he was only one of many people who were working together to bring an end to polio. At the White House, he had said it very plainly: "...[O]n behalf of all the people in laboratories, in the field, and those behind the lines, I gladly accept this recognition of what each of us has contributed...."

Then something went terribly wrong. Just thirteen days after the Salk vaccine was licensed for general sale, a baby in Chicago became paralyzed. He had received a shot from a doctor. The vaccine had been made by Cutter Laboratories, one of the six companies making the vaccine at that time. The next day, scientists learned that five children in California, also vaccinated with Cutter vaccine, had become paralyzed. On April 27, a large number of California's schoolchildren were supposed to receive shots as part of the National Foundation's plan. Cutter vaccine would be used. No one wanted children to have polio. But no one wanted to destroy the public's faith in the foundation and the Salk vaccine, either.

It was soon found that Cutter had made some batches of vaccine that did not pass safety tests. Cutter had not told the National Institutes of Health about these failures. The surgeon general of the United States, Dr. Leonard A. Scheele, asked Cutter to recall the vaccine it had put on the market. The California vaccinations did not take place.

Some batches of Cutter vaccine did have living poliovirus in them. It was discovered that the company had not followed Salk's exact methods for killing the virus. When he heard of the crisis, Salk told reporters that a thorough study would have to be made. He agreed that it was reasonable to stop vaccinating children. More cases of polio from Cutter vaccine were reported from Idaho.

This was a real crisis, but Salk never lost faith in his vaccine. He knew the problem had to lie in the way Cutter's workers had prepared the vaccine. Salk was close to losing everything. When vaccinated children began dying, the Salk vaccine might be blamed. Then all the vaccinations could be stopped for good!

Meetings were held. The top polio researchers in the nation studied the Cutter problem. They wanted to make sure nothing like it ever happened again. A new committee was formed: the Special Committee to Consider Problems Related to Poliomyelitis Vaccine. At one point in the discussions, some of the scientists (including Sabin and Enders) suggested that the Salk vaccine should never be used again.

Every day, more cases of polio were discovered. But all these cases were caused by Cutter vaccine. Millions of shots had now been given using Eli Lilly and Parke, Davis vaccine. No problems had come up with these companies. It was finally discovered that almost half of all the polio vaccine made by Cutter did have living virus in it.

On May 7, 1955, the surgeon general of the United States stopped all polio vaccinations. But, within a week, the vaccines from Parke, Davis and Eli Lilly were approved for use again.

With the help of many scientists, new methods of getting vaccine to physicians were developed. A rule was made that all batches of vaccine, whether or not they passed safety tests, had to be reported to the government. On May 27, the surgeon general announced that all vaccinations could begin again.

Discussions continued during the spring of 1955. In June, a group of physicians and scientists met with a government committee. They were trying to decide if the government should pay the costs of vaccination. Should vaccine be given free to young people who did not have the money to pay for it? Again, the scientists talked about the safety of the Salk vaccine. Albert Sabin was there. He wanted the vaccination program stopped. He believed the strain used in Salk's type 1 vaccine was dangerous. Sabin and his supporters lost the vote. O'Connor told reporters it was time to "get on with the job the American people want done." He said he was afraid the Salk vaccine might be talked to death.

Basil O'Connor had started buying vaccine before anyone knew it would be truly useful. The national field trials had shown that the schools made it easy to vaccinate large numbers of children. O'Connor had a plan to make vaccine available to people who needed it most. He was thinking of the children who had received placebo instead of vaccine during the field trials. Of course, he also wanted vaccine ready for the children who had received no shots—and the vaccinated children who were ready for booster shots. The rest of the foundation's supply would be given to about 7 million schoolchildren in grades one and two.

The vaccine, bought with National Foundation funds, belonged to the people who had sent in their money. So there would be no charge. Also, O'Connor decided that unpaid volunteers would give the shots.

But the government would not go along with O'Connor's idea. Vaccine, given for free? What about the nation's physicians? Officials said people would soon expect all vaccines to be provided for free.

Throughout the summer and fall, the American Medical Association insisted that the Salk polio vaccine should be handled like any other new medicine. People should go to their own physicians and get their shots. The government should not have to make polio vaccine free to every American.

Eventually, Congress passed a law that created a fund of $30 million. States could draw on this money to buy vaccine for people who could not afford private physicians. The foundation carried on with its vaccination program in the meantime, giving vaccine to as many children as possible, as quickly as possible.

In 1955, there were 25 percent fewer cases of polio than usual. In 1956, polio was still around. Several epidemics took place. In Chicago, 1,100 cases were reported. Still, the total number of people who had polio was going down. That fall, the U.S. Public Health Service announced that no child who had had three shots of Salk vaccine had died of polio in 1956.

Jonas Salk spoke at an AMA meeting in Chicago in January 1957. Along with others, Salk advised people to take the responsibility for bringing an end to polio. He said people should get their own shots and take care of the others in their families. Now there was enough vaccine available.

During that year, 1957, people finally began to ask their physicians to vaccinate them against polio. Public health officials said they would make sure people with low incomes received the vaccine. But there were still some delays. Salk came up with the goal of vaccinating every person in Pittsburgh under the age of fifty. He wanted this to be done before summer. Some people hated the idea. Many business people took the physicians' side. They felt strongly that people should go to a physician's office and pay for a vaccination just as they would pay for clothes or food. Salk's plan for vaccinating the people of Pittsburgh was not a complete success. Many people there did not get shots in 1957.

But the number of reported cases of polio was going

down. Some of this was due to the herd effect. Many people had been vaccinated, and they did not have polio. As a result, the "flow" of polioviruses from person to person was slowing down. Then polio began to appear in poorer neighborhoods, where fewer people had been vaccinated. When public health officials discovered this, they called for plans that would bring the vaccine to everyone, not just to people who could afford to have their own physicians. The number of cases of polio in the United States went up in 1959. But the people who had polio had not been vaccinated.

The number went down again in 1960, and in 1961 only 1,312 cases were reported. When only 910 cases were reported in 1962, many people believed the disease would never threaten the American people again. Even Salk was surprised at the success of his vaccine. He had never dreamed it would end the problem of polio in such a short time.

And then a strange thing happened. Albert Sabin's long-promised vaccine came on the market. Suddenly a huge new campaign to fight polio was on! Physicians, the U.S. Public Health Service, the drug companies—all were excited about giving the new Sabin vaccine to every person in the United States.

Throughout the 1950s, the National Foundation had continued to support Sabin's laboratory work. All the time Sabin was trying to stop Salk, O'Connor made sure Sabin was able to do his own research. Sabin first tested his attenuated—but live—virus vaccine on convict volunteers. It was an oral vaccine, taken by mouth. Usually it was put on a sugar cube or in a sweet syrup. People disliked shots, but almost no one minded swallowing a sugar cube.

Sabin's largest test of his vaccine took place in the Soviet Union. The Soviets found it much easier to work with than the Salk vaccine. It was easier to produce, they said. It could be passed out to the people in pieces of candy. This was less costly than setting up clinics where people would come to take shots. Public health officials in the Soviet Union were satisfied with the Sabin vaccine and praised it at scientific conferences. However, they had not done large field trials to prove the effectiveness of Sabin's vaccine. Therefore, they had nothing like the Francis report to support the effectiveness and safety of the oral vaccine.

The U.S. Public Health Service licensed Sabin's vaccine for type 1 and type 2 polioviruses in 1961. In 1962, his vaccine for type 3 poliovirus was licensed, also.

People rushed to take the oral Sabin vaccine. People who had already been vaccinated with the killed-virus vaccine took the Sabin sugar cube. Most clinics charged just a quarter for one vaccination. There was live, but weakened, poliovirus in every drop. Some of the people who took Sabin vaccine did come down with paralytic polio. But many of these people were adults. Therefore, the U.S. Public Health Service suggested that adults should only take the new oral vaccine when an epidemic put them in special danger. For children, there were no such guidelines.

In 1962, Albert Sabin's live-virus vaccine had become more popular than the Salk vaccine. Salk's reply was that the killed-virus vaccine was doing a very good job of wiping out polio—if only more people would go to be vaccinated. But neither the Public Health Service nor the AMA would support him. In vain, Salk pointed out that the only problems with his vaccine were in the vaccination program.

In other countries, like Denmark, where almost everyone had received the Salk vaccine, the number of polio cases was close to zero. Salk said the same thing could happen with Sabin's vaccine. But it worried him that bad cases of polio did happen sometimes when the live-virus vaccine was used.

The Sabin vaccine continued to gain in popularity. The Salk vaccine fell out of use. Salk and O'Connor and many other polio fighters could not understand why scientists in the Sabin camp attacked the Salk vaccine at all. They saw no reason why both vaccines could not be used.

10

The Work Goes On

When he became famous—on the very day Francis announced the results of the field trials—Salk received some good advice from a friend. "Do only that which makes your heart leap," said Dr. Alan Gregg, vice president of the Rockefeller Foundation.

At first, Salk thought he would head a new Department of Preventive Medicine at the University of Pittsburgh School of Medicine. But he knew he would not be happy as an administrator who made speeches or sat at a desk and planned work for others to do. He wanted to go on being a researcher.

In 1956, Salk and his associates did some work with cells of monkey-heart tissue that were acting like cancer cells. They did some experiments with these interesting cells, helped by people who had cancer. As soon as reporters heard cancer patients were going in and out of the hospital in Pittsburgh, they thought Salk was on the brink of a great

Salk in the laboratory at the University of Pittsburgh.

discovery, perhaps a breakthrough in cancer research.

Everything Salk did attracted the attention of the press. He had to explain to reporters that he was still a researcher, doing basic scientific work, asking and answering questions about cells, viruses, and immunity.

The next year, the university turned the Municipal Hospital into "Salk Hall." The latest plan was for Salk to start a new Institute of Experimental Medicine in the building. But again he knew this idea was wrong for him. He did not want to be a leader in the university as much as he wanted to work in his laboratory. He had not changed in character from the eager scientist who accepted the job of typing polioviruses ten years before. Being famous was still very trying for Salk. And not knowing exactly what he should do next was unsettling, too. He kept thinking about regaining the freedom to do research in his own way.

His two brothers were settled in their careers. Herman Salk had become a veterinarian in Palm Springs, California. Lee Salk was a clinical psychologist, well known for his work with parents and young children.

Finally, Jonas got the idea of starting a new and unusual kind of biological institute. It was not to be a school. But it was not to be a moneymaking company, either. He wanted to set up a place where scientists could be creative and work near each other, exchanging ideas and encouraging one another. At his institute, men and women working in many different areas—physics, chemistry, biology, genetics— would be able to do research with no pressure on them except their own need to work.

Basil O'Connor was ready to back his friend. He and Salk both dreamed of bringing together scientists and scholars interested in the behavior and beliefs of human beings as well as in their physical well-being.

The Salk Institute of Biological Studies was founded in 1960 and opened its doors in 1963. The National Foundation had provided the money for Salk to make his dream come true. He probably could not have started the institute if he had not been the man who conquered polio, and he knew that. Discussing his own position as director and fellow of the new establishment, Salk told reporters, "I couldn't possibly have become a member of this institute if I hadn't founded it myself!"

The Salk Institute was built in La Jolla, California, a suburb of the city of San Diego. Salk had the new buildings

President Dwight D. Eisenhower and Dr. Jonas E. Salk, 1960. Salk meets the president on the fifth anniversary of the success of the polio field tests.

designed by a noted architect, Louis Kahn. Of course, some people said he should not have spent money making the surroundings beautiful. But Salk wanted his institute to offer everything researchers could possibly desire. He wanted to attract the scientific world's most talented men and women. The institute had to be a place where they would be comfortable.

Salk himself chose many of the first scientists who came

to work in La Jolla. Among them were Jacob Bronowski, Melvin Cohn, and Francis H. C. Crick (a Nobel Prize winner and one of the three men who discovered the molecular structure of DNA). Also included were Renato Dulbecco (a Nobel Prize winner who became president of the institute in 1989), Edwin Lennox, Jacques Monod (also a Nobel Prize winner), Leo Szilard, and Leslie E. Orgel. Salk had selected outstanding scientists in the fields of mathematics and philosophy, immunochemistry and biophysics, molecular biology, bacteriology and virology, theoretical physics, cellular biochemistry, nuclear physics, and theoretical chemistry.

Salk described his institute as "a place where science and philosophy and human values and the significant in life are artistically combined in a new synthesis that will live and grow."

The institute became the center of Salk's life. He also was adjunct professor in the health sciences at the University of California, San Diego. Salk taught, worked in his laboratory, thought and wrote about his thoughts, and watched over the freedom of the Salk Institute scientists.

The institute was funded by federal grants and by the National Foundation/March of Dimes. The foundation had dropped "Infantile Paralysis" from its name in 1958. It also adopted the important causes of improving the health of mothers and babies and of fighting birth defects. Basil O'Connor remained its president until his death in 1972.

By the 1980s, the institute had grown into one of the world's largest independent centers for biomedical research. Its logo read: "BASIC RESEARCH—KEY TO HEALTH." In the fall of 1989, the institute had a staff of more than 500 workers. More than 200 of these people were doctoral-level scientists (Ph.D.'s). Many were world-famous leaders in their fields. Three were Nobel Prize winners, and others had received such honors as the Presidential Young Investigator Award and membership in the National Academy of Sciences or the Royal Society of London.

Researchers working at the Salk Institute had helped to improve human health in such areas as cancer, birth defects, growth problems, virus infections, and memory loss. The scientists worked with clinical centers throughout the world so their discoveries could be applied to solving the problems of sick people.

In 1990 there were six research centers at the Salk Institute: The Cancer Center, the Center for Human Heredity, the Brain Research Center, the Center for Molecular Medicine, the Center for Plant Biology, and the Center for AIDS Research. In all six of the centers, scientists worked to learn more about biological operations—for example, the workings of the brain, the immune system, the genes, and the AIDS virus.

If they wanted to, scientists at the Salk Institute could devote all their time to research. The institute was not a university, but many men and women came to "learn their trade" there. Scientists from near and far studied new research techniques at the institute. Graduate students carried out their research projects in its laboratories.

The Salk Institute had close ties with research institutes in other lands. Visiting scientists and scientist-teachers helped to keep the institute an exciting and stimulating place. A 1989 bulletin describing the institute summarized its goals and activities this way:

The Salk Institute is a dynamic [forceful] and evolving [changing] institution that is leading the biomedical research community into the twenty-first century. It is making pioneering contributions to the worldwide effort to map and characterize all human genes. Laboratory space is being added to accommodate new faculty members who are leaders in research on the brain, AIDS, the structure of biologically important molecules, and other critical frontiers where major advances are occurring.

After he founded the Salk Institute, Jonas Salk became interested in philosophical writing. Philosophers study what people believe, what they value, and how they live. Salk believed scientists could also be philosophers. He thought they could help other people think and behave more reasonably.

In 1968 Salk's marriage to Donna Lindsay ended in divorce after twenty-nine years. In 1970, when he was fifty-five, Salk married for a second time. His new wife was a Frenchwoman named Françoise Gilot.

Jonas met Françoise when she came to California to see a friend whose husband was working at the Salk Institute. Françoise was a famous beauty who had once loved the great artist Pablo Picasso. In fact, she was the mother of Picasso's grown children, Paloma and Claude. After their marriage, Françoise and Jonas Salk made their home in southern California near the institute.

In 1972, his first book of philosophy, *Man Unfolding*, was published. *Man Unfolding* was the first of four books that Salk has written. These books were not written just for scientists. They were also intended for any readers interested in taking a closer look at human values.

In *Man Unfolding*, Salk wrote about the way biologists think: "The biological way of thought is not an answer but is a way of finding answers. It is a way to examine and order questions so as to be able to deal with them appropriately."

In that book, Salk pointed out that "ideas are not unlike

Françoise Gilot, the artist, and Jonas Salk were married in 1970.

food, vitamins, or vaccines." He wrote that ideas could stimulate "growth and development." He said that because the effects of ideas are "unpredictable," they can lead to all kinds of new experiences.

Salk wrote also about the gravest problems facing humans in the twentieth century, including war:

Can war-making in man be eliminated? This is one of the many questions and challenges still confronting man. It is one in which man has the power of choice.

The challenge confronting [facing] man is to determine whether or not he is able to exercise the choices that will solve this problem, clearly his most important disorder—one that may even be thought of as a self-induced [self-caused] disease.

Throughout his books, especially in his choice of words, it is easy to hear Salk the physician talking!

The Survival of the Wisest was published in 1973. *World Population and Human Values: A New Reality*, which Jonas wrote with his youngest son, Jonathan, came out in 1981. In this book, Salk said that "the well-being of people in other parts of the world is increasingly linked to our own, and our own, likewise, is increasingly linked to theirs." His fourth book, *Anatomy of Reality*, was published in 1983. Here he looked into the twenty-first century, saying, "We need to conduct ourselves so that our descendants will look back on us as having been good ancestors."

Throughout his books, although he wrote about problems and problem solving, Salk remained an optimist. He was a man who looked forward to the future and the surprises it would bring. He expected more good things than bad things to happen. For example, in *World Population and Human Values*, he said he believed that "there seems to be almost an instinct on the part of humans to improve not only their individual conditions but those of others as well."

When Salk celebrated his seventieth birthday, newspeople noted that he was still slender, tanned from the California sun, and "youthful in appearance." He explained that he followed a sensible, low-fat diet and kept fit by exercising.

"I often think of myself as practicing the art of science," he told a writer from *Science Digest*. "At times I see myself as an artist, as a poet. And science is my medium." Indeed, many paragraphs in his books sound like poems. In *Man Unfolding*, he wrote:

The investigation of the atomic nucleus or of outer space is an expression of human nature. These two dark areas are among the many vast unknowns that challenge the human mind and its need to explore. The navigators of days gone by are now those who explore heights, depths, space, the infinitely small, and the magical wonder of the realm of living things.

In 1985, Salk told an interviewer from the magazine *50 Plus* that he was very busy working "at what I like to do." He told of doing research at the institute and speaking to groups of scientists. He was also advising the governments of different countries about public health, especially the health of children. He was working on books and on articles for scientific journals, too.

During the 1980s, Salk began research on a way to make a vaccine to fight AIDS. The disease called AIDS (Acquired Immune Deficiency Syndrome) was first diagnosed in the United States in the late 1970s and early 1980s. AIDS is caused by a virus known as the *human immunodeficiency virus*, or HIV. This virus actually attacks the body's immune system. AIDS is a fatal disease because the weakened immune system cannot protect a sick person from infections. In time, the AIDS patient dies because his or her body cannot fight off other diseases.

People can get AIDS from sex with a person infected with HIV or from contact with infected blood through dirty intravenous needles, which are often used by people addicted to drugs. Also, an infected pregnant woman can pass HIV to her child before it is born.

In 1989, the World Health Organization estimated that 5 million of the world's people were infected with HIV— 2 million of them under twenty-five years of age.

Many health workers felt the most important thing they could do to combat the AIDS epidemic was to educate people, especially teenagers, about AIDS. Some scientists and doctors were searching for better ways to treat AIDS patients and help them live longer. Still others were concentrating on AIDS vaccine research.

In 1987 Jonas Salk applied for a patent on a new vaccine preparation process. At the Fifth International Conference on AIDS, held in 1989 in Montreal, Canada, he reported on experiments with a killed-virus vaccine.

By 1990, he was testing an HIV immunogen on human volunteers at the University of Southern California's cancer center. Salk hoped his immunogen—made of pieces of HIV that had been inactivated—would cause the production of antibodies. The Catholic Archbishop of Los Angeles asked priests and nuns aged sixty-five or older to volunteer to take part in Salk's tests, and this action made news across the nation. Salk's photograph appeared in the newspapers again. People were hopeful that the man who had developed the first successful polio vaccine might be able to help stop the alarming spread of AIDS.

In the 1980s, Salk and Sabin and their polio vaccines were back in the news again—in the Third World countries. Industrialized nations like the United States were almost completely free of the disease. But in Africa, Asia, the Middle East, and Central and South America, physicians were desperately seeking an answer to the problem of paralytic polio. Great numbers of people there had never been vaccinated. In the twenty years between 1963 and 1983,

In the 1980s and 1990s, Dr. Jonas E. Salk continued his research at the Salk Institute in California. He also began developing a vaccine that it was hoped would be safe and effective in fighting AIDS.

seven and a half million Third World people had become victims of polio.

Under these conditions, Sabin's oral vaccine was not as helpful as physicians had expected it to be. For one thing, it had to be refrigerated. That was often difficult in countries with a hot climate. The vaccine did not always work, either. Physician-researchers believed Third World people might be carrying other viruses in their systems that kept the oral vaccine from doing its job. Then, too, the Sabin vaccine had to be given to each person several times over a period of months. In places where people lived far apart and where it was hard for them to travel to a clinic, repeated vaccinations were almost impossible.

The Salk vaccine quickly gained "popularity" in the developing nations. A new Salk-type vaccine was tested, one that would make people immune to polio after only a single shot.

At international conferences, scientists talked about bringing back the Salk vaccine or using it in combination with the Sabin vaccine. The two famous physicians attended as many of these meetings as they could. They discussed polio prevention with officials from other countries, trying to be helpful. (Salk traveled to China in 1985 to discuss immunization and childhood diseases.) But Salk and Sabin still could not really agree not to disagree on which vaccine was better.

What had caused polio to strike so fiercely in this country in the early 1900s? About the time Salk began to work with the poliovirus, scientists found the answer. It was cleanliness. Before people began to worry about germs, many small children had mild cases of polio. They became immune to later attacks, and no one even knew they had had the disease. Thus, polioviruses might be in the environment, but a lot of people had already had it. They did not get sick again, and epidemics could not get started. When living conditions improved in Europe and the United States in the twentieth century, fewer people came in contact with the poliovirus as infants. They didn't get mild cases that would have protected them later on.

Now scientists fear the same thing will happen in the Third World countries. Many people there live under very poor conditions—dirt floors, no clean, running water, no indoor toilets, no disinfectants, few hospitals. Children get polio before they are two, and many of the cases are mild. But what will happen as conditions improve? The children will get polio later, in their teens, and there will be more and more cases of paralysis if nothing is done. Perhaps in the 1990s the Salk vaccine will again be responsible for saving thousands from this terrible disease.

There is another problem about polio that scientists began studying in the 1980s: post-polio syndrome (PPS). It was discovered that older people who had had cases of polio thirty or forty years earlier and had recovered were developing sudden weakness in their arms or legs. Physicians called this PPS. Scientists believe that somehow nerves had been damaged by the long-ago cases of polio. The peak epidemics of polio occurred in the early 1950s. Researchers predict that the peak number of cases of PPS will appear about forty years after that—during the early 1990s.

Jonas Salk has always been a very private person. He did not talk about himself or his family very much. He had not enjoyed being famous, as many people would have done. His picture appeared in newspapers all over the world. Stories about him ran in countless magazines. But this did not please him. Again and again, he told reporters he had not developed the polio vaccine by himself. He explained that many other scientists had taken part in its development through their experiments and discoveries. At one time, he even tried to get people to call the vaccine "the Pitt vaccine." If it had to be named, a friend suggested, it could be named after the University of Pittsburgh. It seemed as if no one took Salk seriously about this or cared how he felt. "The Salk vaccine" was a catchy phrase. And reporters knew people would rather read about a modest young scientist than about a big university.

Other scientists probably thought Salk wanted to take all the credit for developing the vaccine. They turned their backs on him. They would not accept him as one of the group of polio researchers who had worked on the disease for so long. They treated Salk as an outsider just when he had expected to win their approval. Jonas Salk was never invited to become a member of the National Academy of Sciences. (Everyone in this organization is elected to membership by the other scientists.) It was not surprising that Salk was not interested in discussing his life or even in writing about it.

Nearly 58,000 Americans came down with polio in the peak year of 1952, alone. In the early 1990s, it seems as if almost nobody in the United States even thinks about polio. A few cases were reported in Finland in the middle 1980s. A few travelers got a new vaccination just for safety's sake. But they were not really frightened.

Most of today's children know nothing at all about polio. But some of their parents and grandparents remember how life changed during the polio season. One man remembers not being allowed to play with new friends he met in the park. A woman remembers that her mother changed her into a dry bathing suit every time she came out of the swimming pool. Another woman remembers sitting up in bed in the morning when she was a little girl and touching her chin to her chest. She thought this test would show whether or not she had caught polio in the night.

The people who had polio think about polio. And the mothers and fathers of the 1940s and 1950s remember how they worried over their children. They still think about Jonas Salk. Most of them do not care how he did it or why he did it, but Salk came into their lives and took away the thing they feared most. They remember him, and they love him.

Important Dates

1914 Jonas Edward Salk is born in New York City.

1916 First widespread poliomyelitis epidemic in the United States takes place.

1918 Influenza epidemic kills thousands, worldwide.

1921 Franklin Delano Roosevelt becomes ill with paralytic polio.

1926 Salk attends Harris Townsend High School.

1929 Salk enters City College of New York at age 15.

1934 President's Birthday Balls raise over $1,000,000 for polio.

1935 Brodie and Kolmer polio vaccines end in tragedy.

1938 National Foundation for Infantile Paralysis (NFIP) is founded; the March of Dimes begins raising funds.

1939 Salk graduates from New York University School of Medicine; marries Donna Lindsay.

1940–42 Salk interns at Mt. Sinai Hospital.

1942 Salk joins Francis at University of Michigan at Ann Arbor.

1943 Francis, with Salk's assistance, succeeds with killed-virus influenza vaccine.

1944–47 Sons, Peter Salk (1944) and Darrell Salk (1947), are born in Ann Arbor.

1946 Scientists decide modern hygiene paved way for twentieth-century polio epidemics.

1947 Salk accepts position at University of Pittsburgh Medical School.

1949 Enders, Weller, and Robbins grow poliovirus in nonnervous tissue; Salk begins typing viruses for National Foundation.

1950 Jonathan Salk (son) is born in Pittsburgh.

1952 Almost 58,000 come down with polio in United States during peak year of the disease.

1954 Enders, Weller, and Robbins receive Nobel Prize for their tissue culture work; field trials of Salk vaccine involve 1,829,916 children.

1955 Francis report brings good news; Salk vaccine is licensed.

1961–62 Sabin's live-virus vaccine is licensed.

1963 Salk Institute for Biological Studies opens in California; Salk serves as director (1963–1975).

1968 Donna and Jonas Salk are divorced.

1970 Salk marries Françoise Gilot.

1972–83 Salk publishes four books of philosophy and social thought.

1989 Salk addresses Fifth International Conference on AIDS in Montreal.

1990 Salk tests new AIDS vaccine on human subjects.

Bibliography

Books

* Asimov, Isaac. *How Did We Find Out About Germs?* New York: Walker and Company, 1974.

Carter, Richard. *Breakthrough: The Saga of Jonas Salk.* New York: Trident Press, 1966.

Chase, Allan. *Magic Shots: A Human and Scientific Account of the Long and Continuing Struggle to Eradicate Infectious Diseases by Vaccination.* New York: William Morrow & Company, Inc., 1982.

Heintze, Carl. *A Million Locks and Keys: The Story of Immunology.* New York: Hawthorne Books, Inc., 1969.

Klein, Aaron E. *Trial by Fury: The Polio Vaccine Controversy.* New York: Charles Scribner's Sons, 1972.

Peare, Catherine Owens. *The FDR Story.* New York: Thomas Y. Crowell Company, 1962.

* Quastler, Karen. *Jonas Salk*. Castro Valley, California: Quercus Corporation, 1987.

* Rowland, John. *The Polio Man: The Story of Dr. Salk*. New York: Roy Publishers, 1960.

Salk, Jonas. *Man Unfolding*. New York: Harper & Row, 1972.

Smith, Jane S. *Patenting the Sun: Polio and the Salk Vaccine*. New York: William Morrow & Company, 1990.

* Williams, Greer. *Virus Hunters*. London: Hutchinson & Co., Ltd., 1960.

Selected Articles

"Ahead: A Transformation in the Quality of Human Life: A Conversation with Jonas Salk, M.D." *U.S. News and World Report*, December 7, 1981.

Fincher, Jack. "America's Deadly Rendezvous with the 'Spanish Lady.'" *Smithsonian*, January 1989.

Gannes, Stuart. "The Race for an AIDS Vaccine." *Fortune*, December 21, 1987.

Goldberg, Joan Rachel. "The Creative Mind: Jonas Salk." *Science Digest*, June 1984.

Keerdoja, Eileen, with Jane Weisman Stein and Claudia Brinson. "The Polio Pioneers Are Still Busy." *Newsweek*, May 19, 1980.

Krieger, Jane. "What Price Fame—to Dr. Salk." *New York Times Magazine*, July 17, 1955.

Mee, Charles L., Jr. "The Summer Before Salk." *Esquire*, December 1983.

* Readers of the Pioneers in Change book *Jonas Salk* may find this book particularly readable.

"Needed: Nuns and Priests." *Time*, March 26, 1990.

Pekkanen, John. "Are We Closing in on AIDS?" *Reader's Digest*, December 1989.

"A Quiet Young Man's Magnificent Victory." *Newsweek*, April 25, 1955.

Reston, James, Jr. "Interview: Jonas Salk." *Omni*, May 1982.

"Return of Dr. Salk." *Newsweek*, June 11, 1962.

Schwartz, Alan. "Jonas Salk: Champion of Children." *50 Plus*, July 1985.

Siwolop, Sana, with Reginald Rhein and Leslie Helm. "A Tough Old Soldier Joins the Fight Against AIDS." *Business Week*, July 27, 1987.

Stoler, Peter, "A Conversation with Jonas Salk." *Psychology Today*, March 1983.

Wagner, Cynthia G. "AIDS and the Year 2000." *The Futurist*, May–June 1989.

Index

About the Author

Marjorie Curson studied at the Iowa Writers Workshop, received a Woodrow Wilson Fellowship, and earned a master's degree at New York University. She has written many books for teenagers, including her best-selling how-to book, *Forms in Your Future*. This is her first biography. Curson lives in Jersey City and works for a publishing company.

Beginning writers are often taught to write about familiar subjects. Marjorie Curson studied writing with the late Lee Wyndham, who advised her students to "write about things you *don't* know anything about." Curson agrees that research, such as that done for this book, can be very rewarding to a writer, and she believes that the topic of immunology is an especially exciting one.